Jan

# SOLIDARITY
*will transform*
## THE WORLD

# SOLIDARITY

## *will transform*

# THE WORLD

**Stories of Hope from
Catholic Relief Services**

## JEFFRY ODELL KORGEN

ORBIS BOOKS

**Maryknoll, New York 10545**

Third Printing, December 2007

Founded in 1970, Orbis Books endeavors to publish works that enlighten the mind, nourish the spirit, and challenge the conscience. The publishing arm of the Maryknoll Fathers and Brothers, Orbis seeks to explore the global dimensions of the Christian faith and mission, to invite dialogue with diverse cultures and religious traditions, and to serve the cause of reconciliation and peace. The books published reflect the views of their authors and do not represent the official position of the Maryknoll Society. To learn more about Maryknoll and Orbis Books, please visit our website at www.maryknoll.org.

Copyright © 2007 by Jeffry Odell Korgen.

Published by Orbis Books, Maryknoll, New York 10545-0308.

Manufactured in the United States of America.

**Library of Congress Cataloging-in-Publication Data**

Korgen, Jeffry Odell.
    Solidarity will transform the world : stories of hope from Catholic Relief Services / Jeffry Odell Korgen.
       p. cm.
    ISBN-13: 978-1-57075-744-0
    1. Catholic Relief Services. 2. Catholic Church – Charities – Case studies. 3. Church charities – Case studies. 4. Church work with the poor – Case studies. 5. Church and social problems – Catholic Church.
    I. Title.
BX2347.K68 2007
267'.182 – dc22

2007007669

*To my wife, Kathleen*

# Contents

# Foreword

The ministry and work of Catholic Relief Services are directed and guided by Catholic social teaching. That tradition, as ancient as the voice of the Hebrew prophets, as powerful as teaching of the Gospels, and as contemporary as the papal social teaching of the last century, is the foundation, the motivation, and the guiding vision for Catholic Relief Services.

One of the great legacies of Pope John Paul II has been his enhancement and deepening of the Catholic social tradition. Among his multiple contributions was his renewal and renovation of the concept of "solidarity." The term is not new in Catholic social teaching, but John Paul II expanded its meaning and applied it broadly to the changing character of socioeconomic relationships in our era. It is useful to say a word about the *content* he gave to the idea and the *context* in which he saw its application.

In his encyclical "On Social Concern" (*Sollicitudo Rei Socialis*) in 1987, John Paul II defined the content of solidarity as "a firm and persevering determination to commit oneself to the common good; that is to say to the good of all and of each individual, because we are all really responsible for all." The pope was convinced that this principle of moral responsibility should be used within societies and across societies and cultures in international relations.

John Paul II described solidarity as "one of the fundamental principles of the Christian view of social and political organization" (*Centesimus Annus*). In addition to its intrinsic importance, he believed that this basic attitude and conviction were uniquely well suited to the contemporary context of socioeconomic life. The reason for this "fit" between principle and context is the phenomenon first recognized in Catholic teaching by Pope John XXIII, namely, the growing interdependence of human society, both within states and across state boundaries. John XXIII called attention to this phenomenon in the 1960s. By the 1990s, interdependence had qualitatively advanced to a wholly new level of complexity: the appropriate descriptive term had become "globalization," and it posed a challenge for human society as a whole. Globalization knit together the relationships of politics, economics, even cultures in new and highly complex ways. The material elements of globalization — integration further, faster, and farther — could be readily identified and described. But the moral consequences of the process were not so easily catalogued. It was clear by the beginning of the twenty-first century that globalization did not benefit all in the same fashion. Whether one analyzed the life of individuals or states, there were huge differences in the distribution of the benefits of globalization.

This complex process clearly stands in need of moral measurement and moral direction. Providing that direction requires a vision of justice based on the unique human dignity of each person and respect for the basic rights of the person. Solidarity, as defined by Catholic teaching, provides the basic foundation on which the vision of justice arises.

The principle of solidarity not only helps us to envision how a world of growing interdependence can be directed toward greater justice; it also motivates and catalyzes action at different levels of society domestically and internationally. The stories of solidarity in action found in this collection, drawn from many places and many cultures, illustrate the fruits of the idea of solidarity. Here one finds described the engagement of people in a common enterprise, addressing the ancient human challenges of hunger, injustice, and conflict, and new challenges like the scourge of AIDS. The stories are humanly powerful; the lives of men and women recorded here are signs of hope; the products of their generosity move an interdependent world step by step toward greater justice and peace.

Catholic Relief Services, its ministry and work, is woven through these stories. Its very existence testifies to the ancient Catholic conviction that ideas (such as solidarity) are valuable in themselves, but that they also require institutions to give them life across space and time. The work of Catholic Relief Services ties together the generosity of donors, the skill of the professional staff, and the deep commitment of courage and conviction of people across the globe striving to build a better future for their children and their society. This book is not only a great read; it is an inspiring testimony to the human spirit.

*Rev. J. Bryan Hehir*

Parker Gilbert Montgomery Professor
of the Practice of Religion and Public Life,
John F. Kennedy School of Government,
Harvard University

# Acknowledgments

I would like to thank every person who helped make this book a reality. If I have left anyone out of these acknowledgments, I deeply apologize. I am especially grateful to all who helped organize the logistics for the research trips and provided in-country support.

There are four women without whom this book would not have been written: Joan Neal at Catholic Relief Services championed the "Stories of Hope" concept from the very beginning, helped identify the proper balance of topics and countries, and provided invaluable feedback on the manuscript at several stages.

Barbara Myers managed the project admirably, making sure that both CRS staff and I were always well-prepared for the trips, down to the details of what to pack.

My wife, Kathleen Odell Korgen, was incredibly understanding of my absences from the family during 2006 and helped shape the approach of each chapter as we discussed the trips upon my return. Kathleen read each chapter several times, with great patience and insight.

Patricia Odell provided first-rate copyediting and helped immeasurably with the girls while I was away. Julie and Jessica were such good girls while Daddy was on his trips.

The CRS staff proved to be some of the most talented people I have ever met. Both at the agency's headquarters in Baltimore and in the five countries I visited, CRS staff were always warm, hospitable, eager to locate the right interviewees (sometimes adjusting plans to accommodate new ideas), and committed to the lengthy editing process. Hundreds of CRS staff helped make these research trips happen; I would like to thank a few by name: *Mexico:* Erica Dahl-Bredine, Chuck Barret, and Lourdes Aguilar; *Zambia:* Michelle Broemmelsiek, Bridgette Chisenga, Annie Chalwe, Judith Mumbi, Solomon Tesfamarian, and Tina Rodousakis (Baltimore); *India:* Clodagh McCumiskey, Sanchita Banerjee, Rajshree Peter, and Caroline Brennan; *Rwanda:* Sean Gallagher, Gloriosa Uwimpuhwe, Joseph Muyango, Laura Dills, and Paul Rutaysire; *Nicaragua:* Conor Walsh, Jefferson Shriver, and Bill Schmitt.

Staff of CRS partners provided useful background, confirmation of interview details, and translation in the field when interpretive services were unavailable.

Fr. Gene Lauer and the National Pastoral Life Center gave encouragement and release time to complete the in-country research. Gene also provided important feedback on the final manuscript.

A group of friends and colleagues provided feedback on chapters in their formative stages. Their suggestions shaped the final structure and content of the manuscript. I am grateful to each of them for lending their expertise: Pamela Anderson, Ted Miles, Steve Colecchi, Tom Quigley, Michele Gilfillan, Denise Patrick, Suzanne Belongia, Jim Rademaker, Lucio Caruso, and JustFaith group members in the Dioceses of Winona and Grand Rapids.

Susan Perry of Orbis Books offered encouragement and wisdom as well as superb editorial suggestions throughout the research, writing, and editing process. I am truly thankful for the experience of working with such a gifted editor.

Most of all, I am grateful to the people whose stories of hope fill this book. They opened their hearts and lives to a stranger. I am deeply indebted to them and hope that I have retold their stories adequately.

# SOLIDARITY
*will transform*
# THE WORLD

# Introduction

# Solidarity Will Transform the World

*The emaciated boy stared up at me, immobile on his blanket, baking in the Ethiopian sun. He gazed upward from his thin square of fabric, eyes too weak even to plead for food. I stared back, wishing I could help. Then I saw a runner racing, grimacing as he neared the end of a marathon. Someone out of view fed the boy spoonfuls of milk. The boy grimaced like the runner as he struggled to swallow and then stand. Watching the boy lift himself up was as painful as viewing him lie motionless. These words filled the television screen: "We can win the race. Send your contribution now."[1]*

I grew up on public service announcements like these, as common as Schoolhouse Rock segments on Saturday morning television in the 1970s and 1980s. Such advertisements provided a skewed introduction to global poverty. They were fundraising spots — good at conveying the awful fact of poverty in a world of plenty — but too often they portrayed people living in poverty throughout the earth as entirely dependent, without assets to offer the world or even each other.

Images like these, coupled with the mainstream news media's crisis-coverage of global poverty, have created a widespread perception of low-income people across the globe as entirely lacking skills and gifts of their own, dependent on the charity of wealthy nations and individuals just to survive. We give; they receive. "We have everything; they have nothing" is the message. *Send your contribution now.*

I always found that approach lacking. Could a billion people really have so little to offer? When I served as justice and peace education coordinator for the Archdiocese of New York in the late 1990s, I noticed something fresh and different about the images and stories emanating from Operation Rice Bowl, Catholic Relief Services' Lenten hunger awareness and almsgiving program for parishes and schools. Operation Rice Bowl promotional and educational materials often begin with descriptions of famines, natural disasters, or other challenges to human life and dignity, but they quickly segue to stories of hope: what happens when the resources of the Catholic Church come together with the financial, spiritual, social, physical, political, and environmental assets of people living in poverty throughout the world.[2] Even the poorest people have something to offer, and within CRS programs, solutions to global poverty emerge in partnership with low-income beneficiaries. This approach both respects the dignity of poor people and fosters creative responses to overcoming poverty.

CRS roots its commitment to human life and dignity in Catholic social teaching. The late Cardinal Hickey once famously remarked, "We don't help the poor because *they* are Catholic; we do so because *we* are."[3] Catholics feed the hungry because we believe that they possess an inherent dignity that comes from being made in the image and likeness of God. From that dignity proceed specific rights: to food, to health care, and to jobs that pay a living wage, to name a few.

*How* we work with people living in poverty also reflects our belief in human dignity. If we truly believe in the sacredness of human life and the dignity of the human person, we must continually ask if we foster *development* or *dependency* through our ministries. Do we act with the understanding that people living in poverty have resources, or do we view them like the child in the public service announcement, who could not even stand without someone spooning milk into his mouth?

Flowing from Catholic teaching on human dignity is an approach to global poverty called "integral development," a term coined by Pope Paul VI in his 1967 papal encyclical *On the*

*Development of Peoples.* In the 1960s, many in government and the private sector discussed lifting poor countries out of poverty through development; that is, alleviating poverty by growing the economies of the poorest nations. Pope Paul VI was concerned about the language many development experts used because they often limited the conversation to economic terms like "per capita income" and "gross national product." Little spiritual, social, or moral vocabulary accompanied even the clearest of these analyses.

Pope Paul wrote *On the Development of Peoples* to present a Catholic alternative to purely economic models of development. In this letter to the church, one of the highest expressions of papal teaching, he stated, "Development ... cannot be restricted to economic growth alone." Authentic development, the pope insisted, must foster the growth of the *whole* person.[4] Indeed, he cautioned, a sole focus on economic factors might lead to greed, with "dissension and disunity" soon following.[5] Paul stated that defeating poverty and growing in knowledge were the first steps of human development, but he also held out "[expressions of] culture, ... a growing awareness of other people's dignity, a taste for the spirit of poverty, an active interest in the common good, and a desire for peace" as ends for which we should strive.[6]

Not long after Pope Paul promulgated *On the Development of Peoples,* bishops from throughout the globe met in Rome and issued *Justice in the World.* This 1971 statement asserted a "right of development"[7] for poor nations, the human development espoused by Paul VI, but steered in part by low-income people themselves. Development choices appeared to the bishops (many hailing from poor countries) to be too concentrated in the hands of economic elites. They asserted that "all peoples should be able to become the principal architects of their own economic and social development."[8] The bishops also encouraged the church to become a "sign of solidarity" by promoting partnerships between churches in both rich and poor countries, characterized by leadership from people living in poverty.[9]

Sixteen years later, Pope John Paul II offered a devastating twenty-year development report card in his 1987 encyclical *On Social Concern.* Pope John Paul laid most of the blame for underdevelopment at the feet of the Cold War adversaries. The pope reaffirmed Catholic teaching on human development and brought it a step further, articulating the "preferential option for the poor," which he described as a special kind of "exercise of Christian charity." This option or "preference" means that we must always consider how the poor are faring with every decision we make and do all that we can to integrate low-income people into the decision-making structures of society. According to Pope John Paul, just as the Lord has intervened on behalf of the poor throughout salvation history, so should we also try "to imitate the life of Christ. . . . To ignore [people living in poverty] would mean becoming like the 'rich man' who pretended not to know the beggar Lazarus lying at his gate (Luke 16:19–31)."[10]

Those familiar with Catholic social teaching will find the fingerprints of Paul VI, John Paul II, and other architects of Catholic social teaching on every page of this book. Catholic social teaching themes like solidarity; the preferential option for the poor; family, community, and citizenship; rights and responsibilities; the common good; the dignity of work and the rights of workers; and care of God's creation both inspire and shape the work of Catholic Relief Services.[11] The stories of hope that follow offer a kind of mirror to the teaching, reflecting its practice in some of the poorest countries in the world.

During its sixty-year history, Catholic Relief Services has reinterpreted its mission in light of Catholic social teaching several times, including at the end of the Cold War and following the trauma of the Rwanda genocide (see chapter 4). Agency-wide study and discernment has resulted in a greater twenty-first-century emphasis on global solidarity, peacebuilding, and fostering right relationships at all levels of society where CRS operates. In each local context, CRS staff and program beneficiaries assess community assets and challenges using tools derived from Catholic teaching on human development. In addition, the agency has

expanded its relationship with parishes in the United States, fostering solidarity among U.S. Catholics and poor people abroad
through educational programs and legislative advocacy.

*Solidarity* is a current running through each of the projects profiled in this book. The concept begins to answer the question
posed of Jesus in Luke's Gospel: "Who is my neighbor?" (10:25–
37). Theologian Fr. Thomas Massaro, SJ, describes solidarity as a
word that "calls attention to the simple and easily observable fact
that people are interdependent; they rely on each other for almost
all their biological and social needs. . . . We cannot realize our full
potential or appreciate the full meaning of our dignity unless we
share our lives with others and cooperate on projects that hold
the promise of mutual benefit."[12]

Explanations of and references to solidarity can be found
throughout Catholic teaching documents. The word appears
twenty-seven times in the *Catechism of the Catholic Church*, which
describes solidarity as "a direct demand of human and Christian
brotherhood."[13] Countless illustrations of the concept fill the chapters that follow. To read these stories of hope is to enter into a
recitation of the *Catechism* and its articulation of the varieties of
solidarity: "solidarity of the poor among themselves, between rich
and poor, of workers among themselves, [and] between employers
and employees of a business." These stories and the larger social
transformations they represent give life to CRS's visionary motto:
"Solidarity will transform the world." And if, as the *Catechism*
states, "world peace depends on solidarity,"[14] CRS may be one of
our best hopes.

In each of the chapters that follow, Catholic teaching on solidarity and integral development will come to life through stories of
hope articulated by the people CRS serves. You will hear firsthand
from low-income people — in Mexico, Zambia, India, Rwanda,
and Nicaragua — what happens when the lives of people living in poverty around the world are joined with the lives of
U.S. Catholics. You will travel with me to five different projects,
each representing a different model of CRS programming, created

in consultation with the poorest of the poor and implemented through local partners, often Catholic Church agencies.

In chapter 1, you will meet Mexicans who have found hope in the possibility of life with dignity *inside* Mexico through economic development projects along the U.S. border and Catholics in both countries who have discovered new solidarity as one church on a shared international border. In chapter 2, you will encounter Zambians with HIV-AIDS who, like Lazarus, have emerged from the tomb of certain death to experience new life in body and spirit. Chapter 3 will introduce you to women in India whose participation in CRS "self-help groups" brought about both their rise from dollar-a-day poverty and a "new awakening" of capabilities in education, disaster preparedness, public health, and politics. In chapter 4 you will get to know both killers and survivors of Rwanda's genocide who now build peace through forgiveness and reconciliation ministries which challenge the limits we might artificially impose upon Christian forgiveness. Finally, in chapter 5 you will meet Nicaraguan coffee farmers who have begun to triumph over poverty through participation in "the solidarity economy," characterized by CRS-brokered business relationships and Fair Trade certification.

These stories of hope and the human development projects they represent defy crass political categorizations as "liberal" or "conservative." Insisting that the poorest women in India grow savings accounts before receiving a single rupee of microfinance loans is not a conservative ideological tenet; it is simply the most effective method to help these women become self-sufficient. Calling on the U.S. government to fund anti-retroviral treatment for the poor of Zambia who suffer from HIV/AIDS is not part of a liberal political program; it is the principal source of the healing "Lazarus Effect" that CRS fosters in sub-Saharan Africa. For me, this was one of the great lessons of this year-long immersion in global poverty: CRS's stories of hope reveal that both liberals and conservatives have something to contribute to human development, and the end product transcends ideology.

Five countries, five projects: each a story of hope, each an answer to the question "Who is my neighbor?" But be forewarned; these are not all cozy Kumbaya stories of hope, a Catholic *Chicken Soup for the Development Soul.* Some of these travels take us to the furthest depths of human suffering. There were times when I despaired on these visits, as when I sat in the home of a Zambian child with AIDS, watching her shiver in the hot summer air, and when I stood inside Rwanda's Nyamata Church, dwarfed by mountains of human bones that used to be ten thousand people. But as Fr. Ronald Rolheiser, OMI, reminds us, hope is not the same as optimism. Hope is "a vision of life that guides itself by God's promise, irrespective of whether the situation looks optimistic or pessimistic at any given time."[15] Sentiments of sadness and anger, even despair, do not dampen a sense of Christian hope.

Indeed, feelings of anger are an outgrowth of this belief in God's promise. An emotion that might at first seem antithetical to hope is in fact its progeny. Denver Archbishop Charles Chaput addressed this paradox of hope head-on when he spoke to Catholics active in public life at the 2005 National Catholic Prayer Breakfast in Washington, DC, quoting ancient wisdom for a contemporary audience:

> St. Augustine, who had such a deep influence on the mind of our new Holy Father, once wrote that "hope has two beautiful daughters. Their names are anger and courage; anger at the way things are, and courage to see that they do not remain the way they are."[16]

Archbishop Chaput and St. Augustine make the point that hope has consequences. If we live within hope, we overcome "cynicism, indifference, and cowardice"[17] and develop the courage to begin to transform the world.

You will, no doubt, experience many emotions as you read these chapters and discuss them with others using the study guide located at *www.storiesofhope.crs.org.* The remarkable people whom you meet will inspire, even amaze you. The challenges to human life and dignity that they face may also evoke tremendous sorrow.

In these moments, I hope that the wisdom of Fr. Rolheiser and Archbishop Chaput will both comfort and challenge. As you open your heart in solidarity to those you meet in these pages, trust in the Holy Spirit and allow hope's two beautiful daughters to go to work inside you, unlocking anger at the way things are and the courage to see that they do not remain the way they are. *May our solidarity transform the world!*

## Chapter One

# The Golden Kernel

### Building Hope and Solidarity
### on the U.S./Mexico Border

Engracia Guzmán-Cruz stands out in northern Mexico with her sharp Zapotec and Mixtec features, typical of the two ethnic groups most prominent in the southern indigenous zones of Mexico. A short, stocky woman, she migrated to Nogales seventeen years ago from Oaxaca (Wah-HA-Kah), the most ethnically diverse state in Mexico, to northern Mexico in search of a better life. She escaped starvation but found poverty, ultimately working for five dollars a day in the *maquiladoras* (factories owned by U.S. corporations) that dot the landscape of northern Mexico.

Nogales is one of Mexico's most expensive cities. Rents here are almost double those of Hermosillo, just three hours south. The cost of food, utilities, clothing, and appliances are all much more than in the United States,[1] an extra hardship for those living on the minimum wage of $4.50 a day.

Engracia lives in a cardboard house fortified by scraps of wood, tin, and aluminum in the hills of Nogales's *colonias* (unincorporated settlements). She and her husband own the small hillside plot of land that the house sits on, at the top of an outdoor staircase made of discarded tires. The interior of Engracia's house is divided into two rooms: a kitchen and dining area on one side of the house and a bedroom where she, her husband, and their two children sleep on the other. The wall dividing these rooms is a sheet of cardboard with a window cut unevenly through the middle of it.

11

On winter nights in the *colonias*, the temperature gets down to twenty degrees Fahrenheit, but Engracia eschews portable heaters. "Others use space heaters," she explained, but "some of those houses burn down. It's best to just adapt to the climate. We stay warm with blankets."

You will not hear Engracia's story within the shrill debate over U.S. immigration policy. She is a Mexican who wants to stay in Mexico. Thus far, she has withstood the macroeconomic "push" and "pull" factors that have driven 12 million undocumented workers into the United States, the majority of whom illegally crossed the Mexican border.[2] Low commodity prices, Mexico's 40 percent unemployment rate, and its $4.50/day minimum wage offer "push" factors, while demand in the United States for cheap labor serves as an unrelenting "pull" factor.

Currently, 52 percent of the foreign-born population in the United States hails from Latin America. Thirty percent come from Mexico.[3] Crossing the border between the United States and Mexico used to be a simple matter. But in the mid-1990s a new border wall and increased Border Patrol enforcement in Texas and California (Operation Hold the Line) created a new and dangerous phenomenon: the crossing of the Sonora desert in Arizona.

The Sonora desert covers 120,000 square miles of southwestern Arizona and southeastern California, most of Baja California, and the western half of Sonora, Mexico. Temperatures that reach 115 degrees in the warmer months create a constant risk of dehydration, while chilly nighttime temperatures during cooler periods pose the risk of hypothermia. Between September 2005 and March 2006 United States Customs and Border Protection reported 464 deaths along the border, a 43 percent increase over 2004.[4] It is not uncommon to find bleached human bones in the desert or clothes dropped in a straight line, documenting a migrant's descent into madness in the late stages of heat exhaustion.

CRS-Mexico manager Erica Dahl Bredine has characterized the migration relationship between the U.S. and Mexico as "one that forces people to run through a human obstacle course to get here, and if they make it through alive, then they are rewarded with a job." In this challenging context, CRS-Mexico builds hope by developing the human and financial resources of Mexicans, creating alternatives *within* Mexico that give them the option to stay in their country. Many people are aware that Catholic social teaching emphasizes the right to migrate, but the tradition also upholds the right to remain in one's native place. CRS-Mexico nurtures stories of hope within Mexico by developing human and financial assets among Mexicans so they can exercise that right.

Engracia's story of hope springs from the success of a CRS-Mexico project called Bancomún, a microfinance organization of small banks similar to the Indian self-help groups you will meet in chapter 3 but infused with the realities of border life.

### *Bancomún: Micro-Credit in Nogales*

Despite the challenges of life in Nogales, Engracia and her husband, a leather worker, now meet many of their basic needs (food, clothing, school supplies, and medical care) through her growing income as a small business owner. Engracia is a seamstress, and also the president of one of the first microfinance groups formed in Nogales, the Bank of the United. "Microfinance" refers to small-scale savings and loan products that provide an alternative to the loan sharks and *coyotes*[5] who prey on the very poor. In 2004, Engracia met Luis Molina, a bank animator (organizer) for Bancomún, the microfinance institution created by CRS and its partner BorderLinks. Engracia began to pursue a dream of owning her own sewing business through Bancomún because, "I knew that it would help me have a better life *and* work from home." She paused and glanced at her two young children, just arrived home from school.

Successive Bancomún loans ranging from $200 to $300 helped Engracia purchase specialty sewing machines that cut and sew, do embroidery, and manipulate denim and leather. She makes school uniforms, wedding garments, first communion dresses, and some adult clothing. She also embroiders and creates colorful clay ornaments out of cornstarch and water. She shapes the ornaments

*Engracia Guzmán-Cruz shows off apparel that she designed and sewed using funds borrowed from Bancomún (Mexico). Photo by Jeffry Odell Korgen.*

into flowers, dries them, and paints colorful Oaxacan patterns onto the flowers. Engracia showed me samples of wedding dresses and embroidery decorated with these clay flowers. She seemed most proud of the decorative outdoor washing machine covers that she designed and manufactured. There were no samples to show off; she had sold them all.

Outdoor washing machines are everywhere in the dusty *colonias*. Without covers they are vulnerable to damage from airborne dust. Engracia's designs also add beauty to the often harsh landscape. For this last reason in particular, the covers sell exceptionally well.

Engracia's quality of life has improved greatly since she began participating in the Bancomún. Her family now has adequate supplies of food, basic medical care, and, above all, hope for the future. That hope was not always there. "Something has changed in me," she explained. "Participating in the bank has helped me have a vision for the future, to think that this is my work right now, but someday it is going to be an opportunity for my children." Engracia indicated no interest in traveling to the United States except to purchase some supplies (prices are lower in Arizona) and the occasional "breakfast at McDonald's."

The bank's savings requirements have helped her save about $20 a month. When asked what she planned to do with her savings, there was no talk of consumer or household goods, no plans to replace her cardboard walls with cinder block. Like a lot of entrepreneurs, Engracia prefers to invest her profits in the business. Instead of leveling the rocky floor of her home, she has flattened the uneven parcel of land outside, building a supportive cinder block wall to prepare for the construction of her own sewing workshop. There she might employ another seamstress or two, multiplying the hope that the Bank of the United has given her by providing living-wage jobs for others.

Engracia took us on a tour of the neighborhood in a dusty Bancomún van, pointing out the homes that utilize her washing machine covers. We counted seven before reaching our destination, a general store owned and operated by Norma Pacheco,

treasurer of the Bank of the United. Norma started out selling
miscellaneous goods on a board in downtown Nogales. She would
buy small items at the 99 Cents store on the U.S. side of the
border and resell them in Mexico. Then she moved into a small
cinder block building, adding food and larger items. With loans
from Bancomún, she was able to expand the store by 40 percent,
adding inventory like school supplies and gift-wrap. The income
from operating the store has helped supplement her husband's low
wages from a glass installation company.

Norma is one of the few women who own a store in Nogales.
She employs one other woman and is recognized as a community
leader, so people come to her with legal and personal problems,
such as domestic violence. Norma views the banks as an important tool for the empowerment of women. "Here in Mexico," she
explained, "men are very *machista* (embracing excessive mascu-
line qualities). So we have to be dependent on them to give us
money to buy anything. To not have to be dependent on a man,
that makes me feel a lot more secure."

It is the emphasis on helping women that makes the microfinance project unique among CRS-Mexico's projects. Two men
on the Bancomún staff presented complementary perspectives
regarding the project's focus on women. Juan Angulo explained:

> We know from experience that women tend to be much
> more responsible than men. I've seen it! I see how women
> here in Mexico are very good at managing money. Tradi-
> tionally, a man gives a woman an allowance; he might give
> her four hundred pesos ($37.75) and say, "Okay, here's this
> money; you make it stretch to buy food, pay utility bills,
> buy the children's clothing, etc." And I see how they can
> do amazing things with very little money. But it's primarily
> the *way* they are able to manage money. And they are the
> ones that we see who are willing to take a lot of initiative,
> who are more entrepreneurial oftentimes. Right now, 70 per-
> cent of our clients are women, but we want to get that to
> 90 percent.

Luis Molina added another dimension, pointing out that women in developing countries are "double victims of poverty": first because of where they live, and second because of their gender. A history of *machismo* in Mexico and an unmet need for quality childcare keep women out of the best jobs in the formal economy. Even those women with working husbands do not escape poverty; their contributions are often necessary to keep food on the table.

Together with fellow bank "animator" Yvonne Pazos, Juan and Luis promote the Bancomún in neighborhoods and *colonias* in and around Nogales. They make the initial contacts, often via invitations from other bank members, and explain how these microfinance institutions work to potential new members. The bank animators assess people's capacity to repay loans, listing all sources of income and noting their ability to work. They also assess what size loans clients may borrow and repay based on their current business activity and their capacity to expand. Current or previous experience running a business — even selling eggs out of a basket — is vital. The animators obtain references from neighbors and factor in variables like how long the potential clients have lived in Nogales. Ever watchful for evidence of drug paraphernalia, they have learned to spot signs of addiction during these home visits. Many of the banks are located in neighborhoods and *colonias* known for significant drug trafficking.

When a new bank is formed from ten to twenty people living in the same neighborhood, or *colonia,* the animators explain how the loan guarantees work. The first loans are funded by Bancomún. Each member of the bank guarantees the repayment of the other members' loans, which average $200 to $300, repaid over a four-month period. If someone misses a payment, all are responsible for making up the difference. At the end of the cycle, everyone gets new loans, but only if *all* of the previous cycle's loans have been paid. A combination of positive peer pressure and careful selection of bank members has resulted in a repayment rate of 95 percent.

An important moment in the bank's life is its naming. Bank members express both their identity and their hopes through such names as Opportunity, The Dynamite Girls, and The Golden Kernel. In a country whose staple is corn, this last name is especially meaningful. Currently, 1,500 low-income Mexicans participate in 110 banks. By the end of 2007, CRS-Mexico hopes to expand to 7,000 people participating in 650 banks in Nogales and nearby Agua Prieta and Ciudad Juárez. In addition, Luis noted, CRS intends to introduce "solidarity groups" of five to seven women with established businesses who would graduate to larger loans. The bank animators have learned that as the original businesses funded by the banks grow, they require larger loans to sustain development.

To witness a bank in operation, we dropped in on a meeting of "Gaél," a bank named after the two-year-old son of a bank member. Gaél is a new bank; its members were into their second cycle of four-month loans. After each lining up to pay their two-week installment plus savings (the average loan payment is $25.00; the average savings payment is $7.00), the members recalled a meeting held early on for the purpose of determining the bank's name. Gaél ran from bank member to bank member, crawling under tables and spinning around desks, eventually landing at his mother's feet. Gaél's mother, Ludiana, recalled that someone said, "Let's name the bank Gaél," and everyone agreed. It's not surprising: when asked where they find hope, each woman in the circle replied, "My children." The name "Gaél" expresses that priority and provides members with a constant reminder of their hope for the future.

During the short life of the bank, each member had succeeded in growing a small business. Ludiana sells used clothing in an open-air market, clearing $40 to $50 a day after expenses. Nivel has a food stand where she sells hamburgers and quesadillas. María rents plastic tables and chairs for events and sells party supplies. Molina, a diabetic, sells sweet pastries that she makes herself (with no worries about consuming the product!). Each meets a community need, each serves a market, and each has begun to rise from poverty as she has expanded her business.

Biweekly bank meetings provide opportunities to collect loan payments and savings deposits. They also include time for group-building exercises and discussions about community issues, over coffee and cookies. Through this process, the material and human resources of these women grow, but peacebuilding has also figured into the experience. Preexisting conflicts among three of the women in the bank have dissipated over time as a sense of teamwork has grown. Luis views these meetings as essential to the development of the banks. In the future, he hopes to integrate business classes into the biweekly gatherings. Courses on marketing, accounting, and dealing with customers who wish to buy on credit would help these entrepreneurs grow and manage their businesses, he believes.

The group also tries to instill business habits like timeliness among its members. There is a fine system for members who are late or who miss a meeting. A ten-minute grace period allows for varying cultural definitions of "late." Then, fines of ten cents a minute kick in, a very real penalty for people living in poverty. So far, no one has been late or missed a meeting at this bank.

Each of the Mexicans on the staff of Bancomún viewed the microfinance project as a major source of hope on the border. Yvonne explained:

> When I worked as a *maquila* organizer, I realized how little the workers made and how necessary it was for them to do other kinds of work on the side to supplement their income. The people I'm working with in the bank have so much hope and want to take so much initiative. What I've seen is that when people invest a little and it goes well, they get excited and get much more hopeful about their lives and are willing to take more risks and take more initiative. It changes their lives. They realize that they don't have to be dependent on a *maquila* salary!

Luis indicated that the hope provided by the banks also fights despair among people living in poverty. He pointed to Molina, the diabetic sweets peddler, who used to have trouble rising in the morning. "Sometimes she wouldn't get out of bed all day," he said. "When she started her business and learned that she could make a go of it right from her home, she just brightened up and had more energy and confidence. Even if she wasn't feeling well, she would be out of bed and working. Before, she was a loner; she didn't have any communication at all with her neighbors, no relationships. She never came out to talk to people. Now she's really changed."

Molina's story widens the scope of human development: her financial resources have grown; her business skills have expanded; and now her mental health has improved — dramatically. Luis observed that the problem of depression among Mexicans living in poverty is quite widespread, but recovery is common among participants in the banks. "When people see that someone believes in them enough to give them a loan and that they can continue to get larger loans and build up savings, it becomes a source of more hope," he said.

Microfinance projects are growing exponentially throughout the world (see chapter 3). But, as CRS-Mexico manager Erica Dahl-Bredine pointed out, religious and secular aid organizations have until now avoided supporting microfinance projects in northern Mexico.

> There seems to be an assumption that the northern border region isn't nearly as stable as other parts of Mexico or other countries because it has a much more transient population that's often waiting to cross the border into the U.S. to get a better job and better opportunities. Just by the very fact of being on the border, it is thought, people are always on the move. They're generally not originally from the border region. They're from other places and therefore their allegiance is elsewhere. The assumption is that if you invest money in them, they're likely to default on a loan or just not give you the return on an investment that you hoped for.

But the results of this project indicate that many Mexicans at the border *are* looking for reasons to stay. If they can live in what they consider to be acceptable living conditions with family and friends, the push and pull factors of migration lose some of their power. In an area characterized by widespread migration, the outcome of their story is more dramatic than a dangerous desert crossing: they stay at home.

## *El Frente Democrático Campesino:*
## *Hope for the Family Farmer*

Few occupations illustrate the "push" factors of Mexican immigration better than apple farming in the border state of Chihuahua. The affable Oscar Villagrán flashed me a smile as we seated ourselves upon organic fertilizer drums during a barbecue for members of the Frente Democrático Campesino (FDC), a CRS partner. The cookout was hosted by the Molinar family, longtime farmers in Mexico's apple belt, sixty miles southwest of the city of Chihuahua.

Oscar has been growing apples, along with corn, and beans, for thirty-eight years. He is a relatively small producer, growing from 120 to 140 metric tons of apples annually from one thousand trees planted over twelve acres of land. Previously, Oscar was at the mercy of *coyotes,* middlemen who flood Chihuahua at harvest time, looking for desperate farmers willing to sell entire harvests cheaply. Every October, small apple producers flush with their crop try to sell their harvest in Chihuahua at the same time. Since the price of apples dropped precipitously in the 1980s, supply and demand variables have consistently yielded the same result: meager prices at harvest. Oscar has always sold to the first buyer to approach him, for outlays ranging from 15 to 28 cents a pound.

Considering that the average cost of production is 44 cents a pound, apple farming has lately been a losing proposition for Oscar. The crop simply does not provide the income he needs to support his wife, young son, and daughter. He has also been raising a teenage niece since his sister developed a mental illness. Oscar manages to eke out a living for his family from the other crops, but he always lives on the edge of poverty, and decent schools for the children have been out of reach.

Small-scale Mexican apple producers have given up apple farming in droves over the last decade, switching to cattle ranching or abandoning their farms outright, migrating to the United States or cities in Mexico. Such migration has typically replaced one kind of poverty with another. Oscar considered uprooting his apple trees in 2005, but Emiliano Solamente, technical director for the FDC, approached him about participating in a pilot "pledge-loan" project. Emiliano explained the process: at harvest, the FDC would provide Oscar with a 10,000 peso loan.[6] He would in turn pledge not to sell his crop to the *coyote* and to use the loan funds as follows: Three thousand pesos would cover his production costs, paying the harvesters. One thousand pesos would cover the cost of transportation to a cold storage facility that would chill the apples and maintain a relatively oxygen-free environment.[7] Six thousand pesos pay for a four-month lease at the facility. Oscar enrolled and sold his crop in November, when prices rebounded to 70 cents a pound. Had he waited until December, as some of the twenty farmers in the pilot project did, he would have fetched $1.11/pound, over 3.5 times the highest price he ever received.

On average, farmers participating in the pilot pledge-loan program earned 170 percent of previous earnings *after* deducting costs for transportation and storage. They also established a crucial direct relationship with markets in Mexico City and Monterrey, where they are now becoming personally known to buyers (see chapter 5 on "The Solidarity Economy"). When I asked Oscar what he did with the additional profits, he responded like Engracia, speaking only of investments. He purchased a superior irrigation system, hundreds of oscillating drip sprinklers that use less water and require 80 percent less time to operate than his old equipment. He bought a computer to manage the business aspects of the farm more efficiently. He also enrolled his niece in a better school, to ensure that she will be adequately prepared for college. When pressed to identify consumer goods he had purchased, Oscar responded, "Sure, I would like to get a new truck, but I can't do *that!*" Then he paused and added, laughing, "My niece has been asking for a new pair of shoes and a dress for the dances." He shot me a wry look, indicating that he will likely succumb to his niece's petitions.

Oscar is most proud not of his profits, but of his contributions to the local economy. He was able to hire four additional families this year, to help with the harvesting and sorting. These families have already inquired if they will be needed in the fall, and Oscar was most pleased to answer affirmatively. Emiliano has observed this ripple effect in the economy among other farmers participating in the pilot, demonstrating that increased revenue for struggling farmers leads to more farmworker jobs and reduces migration "push" factors on those families.

The success of the 2005 pledge-loan pilot program attracted the attention of the Howard Buffet Foundation and the Broetje Orchards Vista Hermosa Foundation. With new grants from these benefactors, CRS-Mexico economic development coordinator Chuck Barret worked with the FDC to increase the program fivefold in 2006 and significantly raised the quality of their apples — enough to enter the retail market in Mexico. Such expansion offers hope to new participants like the Molinar family, who have farmed in south-central Chihuahua since the 1920s.

Chuck, Emiliano, and I gathered in Isadro Molinar's storage barn, taking in an assortment of relics from over eighty years of farming this land. One of the hundred-foot-long walls serves as a kind of family museum, documenting almost a century of Molinar family farming. Isadro Molinar seemed to be contemplating family history as he held the "E" cattle branding iron, a keepsake from the earliest days of the Rancho Santa Elena. For half a minute, the thirty-nine-year-old stood transfixed before me, gazing at the tool like he understood all too well that the family legacy rests on his shoulders. Gilberto Molinar, Isadro's seventy-one-year-old father, interrupted, pointing with pride to the two-man tree saw that he first used in 1949 and the crude plow and planter that he and his father once utilized to plant corn and beans.

Gilberto related several stories of the ranch's middle years and then shifted to the recent past, explaining that five of his twelve children have illegally crossed the Sonora desert to work in the United States. These adult children have built a life together in Wyoming and send a total of $500 a month to help support the family in Mexico. Remittances like these are the number two source of cash in the Mexican economy, after the sale of oil. Gilberto worried about their dangerous border crossing and now frets that his children can never visit home again. He counseled his seven remaining children to stay in Mexico and find creative ways to boost their income "It's a better life here," he said, "if they can earn *just a little more.* Some of my children have never been back to see their families — for ten or fifteen years! That's bad!"

CRS-Mexico is helping the Molinars achieve their dream of maintaining the family farm for future generations. Isadro, two brothers, and his father are enrolled in the expanded pledge-loan program for 2006. In addition, Isadro accompanied Chuck on a skill-development trip to Washington State, also underwritten by the Broetje Foundation, the charitable arm of the largest contiguous apple farm in the United States. Employing knowledge of the Broetjes from previous work, Chuck encouraged the FDC to send a group of Mexican farmers to Washington to learn pruning and thinning techniques. These methods reduce the number of apples produced but dramatically increase their size and quality.

Emiliano explained that raising the quality of the apples is the key to boosting the economy of the apple belt. "The hook to get people involved in the FDC is the pledge-loan program," he said. "But what is more important is to learn how to produce high-quality apples and organize with other producers for the high-end market." Pruning and thinning techniques will help the farmers increase the quality of their apples, while the FDC identifies and negotiates with buyers in the more lucrative Mexican retail market and, in future years, the organic retail market of both Mexico and the United States.

Currently, the size and quality of the apples produced by farmers organized in the FDC ranks at an average of "3" on Mexico's five-point rating scale. Fours and fives are fit only for juicing. Threes will sell only on the wholesale market. Pruning and thinning will bring most of the Molinars' apples to the "1" category, appropriate for the retail market, and holding the apples in cold storage for a few months will raise the price further. The resulting crop will bring in more cash, despite its lower total mass. Given more time to perfect irrigation, fertilization, and planting techniques, the Molinars might reach two higher categories, which are common in the United States but not in Mexico: "Fancy" and "Extra Fancy." This latter category describes the type of apple one might find in a premium grocery store like Whole Foods Market.

Isadro invited us into his fields to observe pruning and thinning. Pruning refers to the branches. He pointed to minor branches on a tree that he will soon cut off entirely, increasing the flow of nutrients to the main branches and strengthening those remaining. Thinning refers to the flowers and early fruit. Lowering a branch, he counted the fruits; eight immature apples saturated a sub-branch. He removed all but the two largest, which would then draw the nutrients previously shared with the other six. He smiled as he removed the sixth apple. It was the smile of a man who has found a way to push back at the economic forces pushing him.

What would happen to the Molinars without CRS and the FDC? A visit to the tiny Manuel Avila Camacho community, twenty minutes from the Rancho Santa Elena, provided a glimpse of a possible future. I felt as if I were guided by Charles Dickens's "Ghost of Christmas Yet to Come" as we drove past row after row of abandoned handmade adobe houses. Most of the walls of the houses had toppled or caved in during the past fifteen years of outward migration, except in the few inhabited homes. Occasionally we caught a glimpse of a woman or a child. Giant weeds overran whatever landmarks of civil society once existed, including a forlorn public basketball court and community center.

When we reached the ranch of former apple farmer Pedro Torres, I asked him where all the people had gone. "To the United States," he replied. Pedro gave up apple farming a few years ago, switching to small-scale cattle ranching. He explained that all of the farmers in that part of Chihuahua had either switched to beef or moved on entirely. Without CRS and the FDC, this would be the likely fate of the Molinars and the remaining local farmers growing apples, corn, and beans. In most places in the world, land ownership provides at least the possibility of entry into the middle class. Here in Manuel Avila Camacho, land ownership means that you are the last to leave, the one who turns off the lights.

"Are these the shadows of the things that Will be, or are they shadows of things that May be, only?" asked Scrooge. Taking in the ruins of Manuel Avila Camacho, it was hard not to ask the question. Immigration is a phenomenon that obeys economic laws. Migration will be the fate of the Molinars and other family farmers if viable alternatives are not sustained in Mexico. CRS cannot change economic laws, but it can help small family farmers like the Molinars develop the agricultural skills, market penetration, and access to credit they need to compete in the global marketplace. In the process, CRS helps the people it serves build human and material resources to protect the human rights asserted in Catholic social teaching, in particular the right to remain in one's native place.

CRS-Mexico's stories of hope grow not just from efforts to foster better lives for low-income Mexicans, but also through its work to promote solidarity among U.S. citizens and Mexicans. In the six years since CRS-Mexico's border office opened, its two-pronged strategy has produced both economic development projects in northern Mexico and educational immersion programs for U.S. Catholics, to which we now turn. The final stop on our CRS border journey will be Arizona, where Catholic teaching on solidarity is put to perhaps its greatest test: solidarity with neighbors who wish to move in.

## Dioceses Without Borders:
### Building Hope through Solidarity

Barbara Padilla is the kind of parishioner any pastor would wish for. She radiated energy as she ushered me into the parish center at Our Mother of Sorrows parish in Tucson, Arizona, for our interview. Barbara coordinates a flurry of social ministries at the parish and leads a JustFaith study group.[8] Where does this energy come from? I wondered. Is it her red hair or the constant cup of coffee she carries? Neither, I learned; her activity draws from the transforming power of Jesus Christ.

In many ways, Barbara is representative of the Tucson establishment. She lives in the most affluent part of this sprawling city, about ten miles from downtown. She is married to a man of Mexican descent whose family lived in the city before it became part of the United States. A popular local joke lampoons an Easterner who asks an Arizonan of Mexican descent, "When did your people come here?" The Arizonan replies, "We were here when your people came."

For years, Barbara participated little in the parish. She went to Mass, but her involvement stopped there: no activities, no organizational memberships. In 2002 her pastor, Msgr. Thomas Calahane, took a trip with Bishop Gerald Kicanas to Altar, Mexico, a nearby staging ground for migrants preparing to cross the Sonora desert. Msgr. Calahane then organized an immersion trip for parishioners, inviting them from the pulpit to attend. On a whim, Barbara signed up.

In Altar, Barbara was at first unmoved by the presentation on the harsh realities of migrant life offered by a local priest, Fr. René Castañeda. She recalled, "I just thought, 'Oh, that's sad.' I'd heard it before." Then, as part of the tour, she met a group of migrants at a restaurant hideout. She recalled:

> I noticed, off in a corner, there was a lady. She was close to my age, and she was sitting by herself. She looked very sad. I just felt like I wanted to talk to her. So I asked somebody in our group to help me talk to this lady (I don't speak Spanish).

I walked up to her. She was sitting on the floor, and I kind of knelt down in front of her and said hello. I could tell that she was upset, and I asked her if she had children. She said yes, she had four children. She had come from Chiapas, right at the Guatemalan border. She had left her four children in Chiapas with her sister. She was traveling with her brother. From Chiapas to Altar would be like me traveling from Tucson to New York City. She was still in Altar and hadn't even come to the United States yet. She wanted a better life for her kids, but she didn't want to risk her kids. So she left her kids there. She started to cry, and I of course started to cry. I reached out to hug her and she just held on.

For me, that was the moment, the feeling of knowing that *this* is the reason why I came. To see this lady and know that someone would leave their kids like that to try to make something better. That's just not right.

And where was I before? Why wasn't I paying attention? Until you see people and meet people and hear the things that people go through, you just don't get it. At least I didn't. On the way home, after having that experience with her, I thought, You know, these are people who don't have any kind of voice. These are people who die all over the desert, whom people don't know. They read about them in the paper, but there's no story, no connection for people. And if I can be somebody who can try to help people make that connection, then I need to do that for her. On that day, I thought, I'm going to do whatever I can do so that I don't have to see any mom like that again. I didn't know anything about border issues; I didn't really follow any kind of legislation, but I told myself that day that I would try.

Barbara joined the Samaritans, a group that patrols the desert looking for people in distress. They offer food and water, and when medical attention is needed, Samaritans call the Border Patrol.

She also began to sell JustCoffee, a Fair Trade–certified coffee grown in Chiapas, Mexico, and supported by CRS.

Barbara was one of the first to organize a coffee sale in her parish. "I thought, 'This is something I can do! I can sell coffee! I drink coffee twenty-four hours a day!' she explained. 'Coffee is something that I know!'" Barbara brought fifty pounds back to Tucson. At the first parish sale, the coffee quickly sold out and she took orders for over one hundred additional pounds. Some purchasers confided, "I don't drink coffee. I'll give it away. I'll buy it if I know that it will keep *them* there." Barbara tries to respond in a positive way to these parishioners. "I say, 'That's our goal, but you need to understand *why* people choose to come.'" She does not argue; she simply utilizes the moment to tell her own story of solidarity.

In addition to working with the Samaritans and promoting JustCoffee, Barbara also leads parish visits to Altar modeled on her first trip. The visits are a significant part of a CRS-facilitated project called Dioceses Without Borders. In 2003, the bishops of Tucson and Phoenix signed a covenant with the archbishop of Hermosillo, Mexico, to coordinate pastoral ministries and promote border justice and solidarity activities. The three partner dioceses organize trips to Altar to raise awareness about migrants and promote solidarity among Americans and Mexicans. Selected parishes, leaders of other religious denominations, and local officials are targeted, to develop what Erica Dahl-Bredine calls "multipliers of testimony."

Most of these trips draw Catholics who resolve to approach the visit with open minds, but on one recent visit to Altar, Barbara was fearful of the outcome. She explained:

> We went with a group from Our Lady of the Valley in Green Valley, Arizona. It's a retirement community. They were mostly negative. I thought, "This trip is *not* going to go well!" But when we went down there and they talked to people, they were very different. It was because they talked to migrants who said, "You know, I don't want to do this either,

but what would you do? If this was your family, what would you do?"

Since the trip to Altar, the parish now sells JustCoffee. The church also held an educational "border fair" attended by over two hundred people. One outcome of the border fair was a new ministry in which the same parishioners that Barbara worried about prepare packs of Gatorade, cheese, and crackers for the Samaritans.

In addition to the ministries Barbara works with, Dioceses Without Borders brings together pastoral ministers from each of the participating dioceses for planning and relationship building. Joanne Welter, one of the original architects of the partnership, said that the idea for the Dioceses Without Borders project emerged from conversations with CRS about the Diocese of Tucson partnering with an overseas diocese. Joanne clarified why the Tucson diocese ultimately partnered with its Mexican neighbor:

> As a CRS diocesan director, I am aware that several dioceses in the United States partner with dioceses "overseas." In considering who the Diocese of Tucson would partner with, I expressed the idea that "overseas" is an hour from my office, across a desert!
>
> I joke that this is not a partnership, but a *marriage*, because of the geographical ties. In other CRS partnerships, folks travel every year or few years to meet with their partner diocese. In this partnership, we meet every other month, and we seek ways to benefit all of the dioceses through education, spirituality, social action, and relationship building. We are one church on a shared international border. That is the difference in our model of global partnership.

Shortly after the Dioceses Without Borders partnership was founded, the Diocese of Phoenix joined. Bishop Thomas Olmstead noted that even though the Phoenix diocese contained no border cities, local challenges mirrored Tucson's. Two Dioceses Without Borders conventions for local pastoral ministers have been held, the first consisting of relationship-building activities, the second exploring implications for joint ministries.

One of the success stories of the partnership has been the development of joint youth ministries. Teresita Scully, youth minister for St. Elizabeth Ann Seton parish in Tucson, enlarged her parish's youth ministry to include mission trips across the border to help *colonia* residents repair homes and tell their stories. In turn, youth from Mexico crossed the border for *encuentros* (youth conferences) in the United States with teens from Arizona. Despite the linguistic barriers, the youth nevertheless developed relationships through shared experiences of the Rosary, Stations of the Cross, Mass, and music.

The same young people have participated in Dioceses Without Borders *posadas,* reenactments of the Holy Family's journey to Bethlehem. Busloads of teens traveled from Phoenix and Tucson to Nogales. They gathered on the American side of the border in an area where the wall softens into a mesh fence. On the other side, a group of Mexican youth assembled. The two groups faced each other across the mesh and sang religious songs to one another. The U.S. teens streamed through the border gates, and the united church processed through the streets of Nogales. The youth carried signs reading "Dioceses Without Borders Respects the Dignity of All Persons." A group of migrants joined the procession. They ate a meal together and broke a piñata. Then the youth reenacted the story of the Holy Family. One of the migrant men portrayed Joséph.

After the play, the young people gathered in smaller groups to hear the stories of migrants. Teresita explained that "the kids ask where migrants came from and how they got there, but they are most interested in why they left their homes." Like the visits to Altar, the *posadas* succeed in building relationships, promoting solidarity, and fostering social analysis among the youth and their adult leaders.

Both the Americans and Mexicans who participate in Dioceses Without Borders find that their stereotypes of the people on the other side of the border are challenged. Fr. Cayetano Cabrera, a pastor in Agua Prieta, stated that his views of U.S. citizens changed as a result of participation in the partnership:

> As a Mexican, I always thought of the Americans or the United States as very bad, as people who are racists, who are only interested in money, who have no heart, and this changed a lot through this process. I see that there is a lot of saintliness in the people of the United States, that God is very present in their lives. There are many people in the U.S. who have very open minds, who are very committed and who are willing to sacrifice and give of themselves. Through this I've been able to love the church even more and become more committed to my priesthood.

Fr. Ivan Bernal, a Mexican priest who ministers to Central American migrants apprehended at the Mexican border, reported a similar experience. He maintains that the face-to-face experience with U.S. citizens through Dioceses Without Borders has offered him hope that immigration justice is possible:

> My hope lies in the people who are becoming educated and aware about this. I believe that these are the people who are going to change things and show that we don't need this wall holding us apart from each other. God made us brothers and sisters; there should be no division between us. We're all one and we're all equal. We are responding to the call of God here, and we're working to build the kingdom of Heaven.

The success of Dioceses Without Borders encouraged CRS to look for a way to export stories of the border to other parts of the United States. CRS commissioned a team of theater students from Villanova University outside Philadelphia to collect stories of the border from the various principals: migrants, Border Patrol agents, ranchers, parishioners, government officials, and even a coroner. The result is a drama that takes into account the complexity of the border. It is neither a liberal polemic nor a journalistic "both sides" account. *The Line in the Sand: Stories from the U.S./Mexico Border* expresses the Catholic commitment to border justice by articulating the positions of multiple players on the border (from actual interviews). Discussion time after the play encourages audience members to utilize the tools of Catholic social teaching to discern policies that will promote the common good. The production begins with the testimony of Lucrecia, a migrant whose bones are discovered in the desert at the end of the performance:

> I love my children. They're why I'm here. A family should be together, no? José already has the two oldest ones with him in Chicago. Years ago, José could leave for a few months to work, and then come back home. But no, not anymore. Now, to go back and forth is too difficult. So we must go to him, to be together. That was not what we dreamed of for our family. [*confused*] What? No, ah. [*composed again*] We never wanted to leave, but there is no work in Sombrette. Only farmers who can't sell their crop, and wives with husbands far away. For two years, he's been gone. I've been without *mi esposo por dos años*. I hate him being there. This was not our dream. . . . No. So I prayed to Our Lady. I prayed she would keep my children safe. . . .

This testimony is quickly followed by the reflections of a Border Patrol agent:

> I mean, it's not like we want anyone to die, you know. We're trying to help people as much as we can, but our duty is to the United States and protecting her borders. And down here, we have more responsibility than in other regions. The border crossings in Texas and California have been tightened, funneling all the bodies our way. It's not just migration we're dealing with, but also drug trafficking, *human* trafficking; it's all coming toward us. We're the stop in the dam. I mean, they're pushed this way for a reason. All the open space, the desert, it gives us . . . well, response time. In a city, aliens can disappear, just vanish.

I get it, you know? I know that most of these people, aliens, coming across, I know that they're good people. I have kids myself. I'd do whatever it took for them to be safe and healthy.... But among these aliens, and let me be clear on this, let there be no mistake about this, there are criminals, murderers, drug smugglers, terrorists. We've already caught two this year that were on the U.S. Terror Watch list. We're not just rounding up poor farmers and sending them back. There's a bad element in there.

The play continues in this vein, stitching together various border perspectives. The composite picture portrays a broken system in need of thoughtful, compassionate repair. When *The Line in the Sand* concludes, the audience joins in a discussion with CRS staff and the actors about the play, the current situation on the border, and how viewers might take action for border justice. Colleges, high schools, and parishes far from the border are thus able to encounter stories of the border and engage the public policy questions at stake without costly travel. *The Line in the Sand* production multiplies the stories of hope through solidarity that Dioceses Without Borders creates, and a recently filmed DVD has made the play accessible to every parish and school in the United States.[9]

*The Line in the Sand* and the other three CRS-Mexico border programs stand together as a peacebuilding effort as much as an integral human development project. The banks and the FDC develop material assets, business acumen, and agricultural skills, addressing head-on the desperate forces driving migration into the United States. The Dioceses Without Borders partnership offers an immersion into border life that develops the capacity for solidarity among participants. The result is a comprehensive effort that helps both U.S. and Mexican Catholics alter the formulas of violence that, until now, have equaled over two thousand deaths in the desert and a terrible resentment of migrants among U.S. citizens. CRS-Mexico has facilitated important steps toward border justice in these short five years — among them the growing realization among Catholic leaders that they are one people, one church, living with hope on a shared international border.

---

### For Reflection

*You shall also love the stranger, for you were strangers in the land of Egypt.* (Deut. 10:19)

- How are U.S. Catholics called to support people at the U.S.-Mexico border?

Please go on-line to *www.storiesofhope.crs.org* for a comprehensive study guide.

# Chapter Two

# The Lazarus Effect

*Fighting HIV/AIDS in Zambia*

In the fall of 2004, a mile and a half below the surface of the earth, Ken Mwansa collapsed into the arms of a fellow drill-operator in Zambia's rough-and-tumble Copper Belt. When he awoke in Wusakile Hospital, he suspected that he may have contracted malaria, but he feared the worst: HIV/AIDS. The pandemic had already orphaned nearly 1 million Zambian children, and he worried the virus might soon render his four sets of twins fatherless.

Before 2005, an HIV/AIDS diagnosis in Zambia meant certain death. In an interview at the start of my March 2006 visit to the country, CRS-Zambia director Michelle Foust Broemmelsiek described a common experience for Zambians with AIDS:

> We have stories of people with HIV/AIDS who, because funerals are such a financial burden on their families, try and scrape up enough money to purchase their own coffin while they still live. Then, as the disease progresses, they sell everything, because they can't work. They use up everything they have, and in the end, they don't have anything left except the coffin, the only piece of furniture left in their house. They're sleeping on top of their coffin, waiting for death.

During my visit to Zambia, I heard many stories of these grim deaths, which reliably came within months of diagnosis. The best a group like Catholic Relief Services could do in the early years of this century was to partner with local dioceses and health care organizations, providing nutrition and simple treatments for the many opportunistic infections that accompany AIDS. There was no effective treatment for the virus itself.

After testing Ken for a variety of maladies, doctors at the mining company hospital diagnosed him with both malaria and AIDS. While bedridden, Ken lost sixty-eight pounds, and his CD4 count, a barometer of immune functioning, fell to 196, far below the normal level of five hundred to fifteen hundred cells per cubic millimeter of blood. If Ken had collapsed even months earlier, he could only have hoped to die with dignity and pray that relatives would care for his eight children. But hope arrived in the form of CRS-Zambia and its partners, through new nutrition and health programs funded principally by the U.S. government, via the President's Emergency Plan for AIDS Relief (PEPFAR) with additional support from individual contributions to CRS. PEPFAR, approved by Congress in 2003, authorizes spending $15 billion over five years on the prevention and treatment of global AIDS, tuberculosis, and malaria, with a special emphasis on the countries of Africa and the Caribbean.

In CRS-Zambia's records, Ken is referred to as Case 001, an indication of just how close he came to death. He was the first Zambian to receive American anti-retroviral drugs, or ARVs, through Catholic Relief Services. These are the drugs responsible for the return to health of millions of people living with AIDS in industrialized countries. ARVs include such drugs as Zidovudine, Efavirenz, Lopinavir, and Nelfinavir, to name a few. When taken together, in precise combination with the requisite foods, ARVs inhibit the replication of HIV, enabling a person with AIDS to live a remarkably normal life.

The complexity of taking ARVs requires additional programmatic supports. A CRS-partnered "Home-based Care" volunteer visits Ken weekly to deliver high-calorie, high-protein nutritional supplements and discuss the supports he needs to follow the treatment regimen. Without this supportive adjunct, led by ordinary Zambians trained by CRS, the medications would not produce such dramatic results; malnutrition and forgetfulness would stymie their effectiveness.

Until now, it was impossible for Zambians (and many others living in developing countries) to access ARVs. Currently, 17,500 Zambians participate in AIDS Relief, the CRS-Zambia ARV program, while 37,500 participate in ARV programs administered by other organizations, which employ cheaper, Indian-manufactured generics.[1] While this number is far smaller than the estimated 160,000 Zambians with AIDS symptoms,[2] it is a dramatic start, a far more hopeful scenario than purchasing a coffin and waiting to die.

But rampant poverty and malnutrition in sub-Saharan Africa stymie the effectiveness of these medicines. In Zambia, 73 percent of the population lives in poverty and 47 percent of the children show signs of stunted growth. The country ranks 161st out of 177 countries in the world in terms of per capita income. Within that ranking, Zambia is the poorest peaceful country in the world.

This was not always the case. When Zambia achieved independence from Rhodesia in 1964, it was a middle-income country. Devastated by droughts and natural disasters, fluctuating copper prices, and a disastrous experience with socialism, Zambia descended into poverty in the 1970s. A massive auction of state assets to multi-national corporations placed the nation's copper supply in the hands of foreigners. Many of the remaining financial resources in the country have been frittered away by government corruption. Now Zambia's poverty and food insecurity appear intransigent, exacerbating an already devastating pandemic.

Ken appeared fit, though gaunt, when I met with him at his sister's home near the city of Kitwe. The lack of electricity in the home became obvious as the house dimmed with the setting of the sun. Square holes in the concrete walls served as windows, allowing easy access for malaria-bearing mosquitoes. After taking ARVs for months, Ken was bullish about returning to full-time employment. "I can work!" he insisted. Although he has been warned by his doctor to avoid below-surface duties, where tuberculosis looms as a constant threat, he was eager to go back to productive labor, any sort of job, even if it meant taking a pay cut.

Ken's eight children darted around him as he spoke. They, too, are part of his treatment regimen. He explained, "The children ask me, 'Father, are you taking your medicine?' Or if I am asleep, they press something against my ear: 'Father, you are not drinking your medicine; stand to drink!' "

At each house, Home-based Care volunteers from CRS partner organizations select someone in the household to remind the client to take his or her medicine. Taking ARVs properly requires attention to detail that people living with AIDS often cannot muster. Sometimes these "buddies" are parents or siblings; sometimes they are neighbors or friends; sometimes they are spouses. In cases like Ken's, where spouses have deserted or died, and friends and neighbors shun the person with HIV, children are the best supports available.

Ken contracted HIV from sexual contact outside of marriage. When he was diagnosed with AIDS, Ken's wife moved out and into her parents' home, leaving the children with him. Angry about her husband's infidelity but unwilling to bring herself into a clinic for testing, she developed symptoms of AIDS in late 2005. She is now far sicker than Ken. Although she was furious with Ken for putting her at risk for HIV, she never overcame her denial, even refusing treatment. Dementia has set in, and relatives are trying to get her tested, aiming to enroll her in an ARV program.

Ken also experienced stigmatization from friends and neighbors. His collapse was a public event, witnessed by eleven colleagues at Mopani Copper Mines, who quickly spread the rumor that he had AIDS. The isolation was immediate. Friends and neighbors ran when he approached; no one would eat with him. He became cut off from all of the former supports in his life, a stranger in his own neighborhood. Demoralized and anxious for a fresh start, he moved in with a supportive older sister in another Kitwe compound.[3] She helped Ken treat his illness and mind the twins. He began attending a local Catholic church with his children. Recently, the pastor asked him to lead the choir.

As Ken spoke about his renewed interest in church, I asked him how his life was different now, how he had changed. He replied,

I can't die anymore. Before, I used to womanize. I used to have a lot of women here and there like everybody's doing. So after what I have gone through, that I have stopped. I've repented now, as a prodigal son. He repented once, and now I have. As a Catholic, I think that God understands me, that he will pardon me for what I have done.

Thinking that a choir director might enjoy an opportunity to sing, I asked Ken to sing his favorite song. With only a pause to inhale, he began singing in Bemba, one of seventy-two tribal dialects in Zambia:

*Wapangile umulu tata wapanga na Bantu waapanga na kasuba,*
*kalesanika monse tata cilempapusha. Tatacilampelenganya*
     *kakutashe*
*nkakuylumbe mu ntambi.*

You made the world, the people and the bright sun which
     shines over us.
It touches my heart. Let me adore and praise you, Father.

*Nkakutashe tata we mulopwe, iye!*
*Nkakutashe tata we mulopwe!*

Let me praise you Father!
I will forever praise you, Father!

*Wapangile umulu tata, wapangile nabantu, wapangile naine.*
*Wapanga nakasuba kalesanika monse tata.*
*Cilampapusha tat, nkakutashe nkakwimbile muntambi!* (x2)

Creator of heaven, Creator of all beings, Creator of the sun,
You then added me to your creation.
It touches my heart.
I should give you praise and sing songs of praise and worship.
I should worship you as in psalms and parables.

*Nkakutashe tata we mulopwe, iye!*
*Nkakutashe tata we mulopwe!*

Let me praise you Father!
I will forever praise you, Father!

As he finished, I heard the verses of a much older song, "I shall not die, but I shall live, and recount the deeds of the Lord" (Ps. 118:17), and knew that Christ was alive and healing lepers in Zambia.

### *The Lazarus Effect*

Listening to Ken speak about the worst of his illness, it seemed a miracle he was alive at all. The Copper Belt's Catholic Irish-born bishop, Rt. Rev. Noel O'Regan, described it as just that: a miracle. Seated in an unassuming office complex that looked more like a struggling retreat center than a chancery, Bishop O'Regan explained:

> Some people have called it "The Lazarus Effect," referring to Christ raising Lazarus from the dead in chapter 11 of the Gospel according to John. So many people who were about to die are now living active lives. For me, "The Lazarus Effect" means that someone who was as good as dead, about to expire, had the blessing to find someone who could open the way for them to take these drugs. The result has been miraculous. You don't often ascribe miracles to drugs, but in this case it is really so wonderful that you could use the word "miraculous."

Bishop O'Regan observed the Lazarus Effect in a member of his own staff, a woman who was expected to die within a week of diagnosis. She now operates heavy equipment for a copper mining company. She received generic Indian ARVs through a program in a miners' hospital. Nutritional supplements and home visits from CRS partners helped ensure that she took the medicine properly.

As in Ken's case, the miracle of ARVs occurred not simply through the action of the drugs, but also through the intervention of Home-based Care providers partnered with CRS. These volunteers

visit people living with AIDS to ensure that their nutritional needs
are met. They also make sure that clients have the necessary
supports to take their medications on time and with the right
foods. The Lazarus Effect therefore springs from the intersection
of the medical and financial resources of the U.S. Catholic Church
and the American people (via the PEPFAR initiative) and the
human resources of the people of Zambia, though institutional
partnerships and relationships with the individual Zambians who
volunteer.

A Zambian proverb states: *Umunwe uno tausalando,* "You need
two fingers to pick up a louse." The expression means that serious
problems cannot be solved by individuals; they must be tackled
by people working together. While many stigmatize people with
AIDS, others gather to find ways to be supportive.

Bishop O'Regan explained that he has been most impressed with
the commitment to visiting the sick among Zambian Christians,
who make up most of the population:

> They visit the sick to such an extent that sometimes it's a
> little overpowering. If you go to any of the hospitals here at
> visiting time, if you're going against the flow of people, when
> that gate opens, and the visiting hours begin, there is no
> way you can come down those stairs; they are coming up and
> there are hundreds and hundreds; there might be a thousand.
> It's like a rush of people coming out of a football stadium.
> Sometimes you're lucky if you can just see the patient, over
> their heads.

Bishop O'Regan believes that 90 percent of hospital visitors come
to comfort friends, relatives, and neighbors. The remaining 10 percent are making general calls on the sick. A visit to Kitwe's
Central Hospital bore this insight out. While many Zambians with
HIV/AIDS die lonely deaths at home, no one was ever alone during
hospital visiting hours.

By the same token, there are always plenty of volunteers for
the various CRS partner HIV/AIDS programs. Some are moti-
vated by the Gospel; others are moved by the suffering that they

see. If nothing else, all are aware of the Zambian proverb *Usunga teshibikwa.* "It is difficult to know the person who will take care of you when you are in need," meaning that you should help others today because you may need their help tomorrow. Without CRS, well-meaning volunteers would likely alleviate some suffering, but they would lack essential training in a variety of help-related topics, such as the role of nutrition when taking ARVs, proper responses to stigmatization, and the true means by which HIV is spread. Justina Mwambaba is a volunteer caregiver who lives in a low-income compound of homes outside of Kibungo, Zambia. She related her experiences to me at a local health clinic, which partners with CRS to provide Home-based Care.

In addition to the basics of the CRS training, Justina noted the pro-active nature of Home-based Care. Volunteers are taught to look out for neighbors who quietly waste away with no one to look out for them. The caregivers then invite people with AIDS into the AIDS Relief (ARV), Home-based Care, and Orphans and Vulnerable Children programs.

Justina became involved in the Home-based Care program out of a mixture of altruism and *Usunga teshibikwa.* "There were quite a number of people infected with HIV who were just abandoned and were not being looked after," she recalled. "So when the call came in the church to join and help others, I answered. It is also true that we may help others today, but tomorrow, if I am infected, someone else will look after me."

Justina provides in-home care each week for fifteen people who live in her compound. The tasks vary with each client. She might help with household chores. She might bathe a client. She might cook for a person with HIV/AIDS and his or her family. In each home she assesses needs and tries to determine how to meet those needs. Is the client signed up to receive PEPFAR food supplements? Are the children enrolled in the Orphans and Vulnerable Children program? Is someone in the home monitoring compliance with the ARV regimen?

Justina's husband is a security guard, one of only 13 percent of Zambians employed in the formal economy. Without his steady paycheck, she would not be able to volunteer. Still, money is tight, and they often discuss her getting a paying job. In general, the volunteers in the various CRS-supported programs are just as poor as the clients, which helps to build trust, minimizing the cultural learning curve for volunteers.

### *Soldiers for Life*

It is difficult to visit Zambia and not feel as though you are witnessing a nation at war. Despite Zambia's peaceful traditions, the body count is undeniable. The hospitals are full of the dying, brought in wheelbarrows by concerned neighbors. CRS country director Michelle Foust Broemmelsiek described the cancerous growth of Lusaka's public cemetery as a phenomenon not known in the modern world outside the experience of war:

> In the cemetery, you will find, starting in the morning, there are funerals going on. They have a bunch of gravediggers, and they are digging graves. Before those gravediggers finish the last grave in the row, the people are there to bury their dead. Before they finish that row, they are starting on the next row. The cemetery grows that day by as many graves as the cemetery gravediggers can dig.

If the battle against HIV/AIDS is a war, then some of the most tenacious fighters are people living with HIV. CRS's Bridgette Chisenga is one of those soldiers. Born and raised in Chingola, Zambia, she moved to neighboring Botswana to live and work as an expatriate teacher in the 1990s. In 2002 she began losing weight, feeling fatigued, and developing unusual infections. She tested positive for HIV and, outside of working hours, withdrew into her home. She recalled:

> I wouldn't talk. I wouldn't even utter the word HIV, let alone let it be known that I was HIV positive. I would just be embarrassed — what would people think of me? I would

not even tell my family what was wrong with me. I would say, "I have been bewitched," or "I have cancer."

When one gets HIV infection, there is that withdrawal. You actually hide away from people. And people start pointing fingers at you, name calling, and so forth. Stigma comes not only from your friends but also from the community, even your relatives. You even stigmatize yourself by withdrawing. I stigmatized myself to the extent that I almost died in my own house. I didn't want anyone to see me.

Bridgette was fortunate to be living in Botswana, where ARVs had become available. She responded to treatment and began to regain weight. She overcame her isolation and self-stigmatization and returned home to Zambia in December 2003. "I asked myself," she said, "What am I going to do now? I am infected; I am on ARVs. I decided to go into HIV prevention."

Bridgette channeled her anger at stigmatization into outreach work with commercial sex workers, fishermen, and truck drivers through a secular program called Corridors of Hope. After two years with that agency, she accepted a post with CRS, as the adherence officer for AIDS Relief. In this work, she draws from her experience with the disease to help other Zambians with HIV. She explained that people participating in the AIDS Relief program need help remembering to take their medicine, but an even greater challenge is making sure clients eat the foods necessary for the medicines to work effectively. People taking ARVs will say, "Sometimes, I tell you, I don't take my medicine. I take the medicine when I have food. Sometimes I look for food and it may take fourteen hours."

CRS staff call this problem "food security." Food security has three dimensions. First, is there enough food available in the country? Did the country produce enough? Second, do people have access to food? Do they have ways of keeping grain in good condition after the harvest? Do they have enough money to purchase needed foods? Finally, are family members healthy enough to utilize the food that they eat? This dimension is especially important to HIV-infected populations.

CRS has responded to food insecurity by promoting the cultivation of drought-resistant crops and hosting "seed fairs" throughout Zambia. In a community seed fair, participants receive vouchers for the seeds they need. Vendors display a variety of seeds that families then choose from, paying with vouchers. At the end of the fair, CRS redeems the vouchers for cash. In addition to running agriculture programs, the agency distributes a high-protein porridge, formulated by USAID (United States Agency for International Development), to Zambians who qualify for the AIDS Relief program. Locating and registering those eligible to receive these supplements is part of Bridgette's job.

Another HIV-infected soldier in the war against AIDS is Judith Mumbi, a nurse by training, who joined our group midway through the visit. Judith guided our driver to interviewees in a low-income compound where she sometimes makes home visits. Judith's story is representative of many women fighting on the front lines against HIV/AIDS.

Judith contracted HIV from her husband, who got it from extramarital sex. Living with the virus led her to seek a position with a CRS partner helping people with AIDS take their medicines and respond properly to opportunistic infections. She believes that her call is not only to treat the sick, but also to challenge cultural norms that allow men to have two or three sexual partners outside of marriage. "As women, we accept this," she said. "My own husband got AIDS and gave it to me. He was in denial. He was in denial until he died."

Judith guided us through one of the poorest compounds in Kitwe to meet Justin Mubanga, a man in his mid-thirties whose ARV treatment is just beginning. Justin lives with his brother and his family. He is no longer bedridden, but still suffers from a tropical ulcer of the foot, a stomach-rending condition to view that requires daily washing with peroxide. Judith selected Justin as an interviewee in part because no health care providers would venture into the compound to change the dressing on his ulcerated foot. Our visit gave her the opportunity to clean the wound and apply fresh bandages.

I began the interview by asking Justin how he was feeling. Dressed in a Dallas Cowboys windbreaker, looking emaciated but alert, he spoke of his recent recovery from tuberculosis and his hope that he would soon return to work. "That foot will have to heal," I thought, as Judith removed the dressing, revealing a large, blood-red ulcer. Justin went on to describe the four medicines that he takes daily, along with vitamins, high-protein cereal, and whatever fruits and vegetables his mother and brother are able to obtain.

The room became oddly silent. Even Justin's four nieces and nephews quieted their play in the next room. As Judith applied peroxide to the ulcerated foot, I realized that I had seen this scene before: she was washing the feet of Christ. As Judith completed the footwashing, I understood that I was observing the most gentle of warriors, a soldier at war with HIV, fighting for human life with charity, compassion, and the tools of her profession, fighting the virus that might have taken her own life, taking the battle to the poorest of neighborhoods in one of the poorest countries of the world. Christ wears a Dallas Cowboys windbreaker here in Zambia, and I was honored to watch one worthy of washing his feet.

### *Lazarus Wants a Job*

The raising of Lazarus from the dead is one of the most dramatic moments of the Gospel according to John. Imagine for a moment that you are at the scene (11:17). The stone to Lazarus's tomb has been rolled away. Jesus stands at the entrance and cries, "Lazarus, come out!" Lazarus emerges, still bound by burial cloths. We do not know what he said to Jesus, but what if he whispered, "Now that I'm feeling better, could you help me find a job?"

This is the question beneficiaries of the AIDS Relief program are asking as the Lazarus Effect takes hold. Esther Mulenga Chilandro is a case in point. A young widow with six children (her husband died of malaria a few years ago), she began to develop symptoms of AIDS in 2003:

I had abscesses all over my body. Because of the sores I had problems dressing up, And even sitting down. I started getting very thin; I felt sick all the time, my body looked grey, and my hair was stringy. I weighed only ninety-two pounds. I went for a doctor's visit and found that I was HIV positive. Then the ARVs were explained to me, and I was given the opportunity to take them.

During her first week on ARVs, Esther experienced strong side effects. Her doctors altered the combination of drugs, and her body tolerated the new regimen much better. Her two eldest children take responsibility for reminding her to take her medication, and the Home-based Care volunteers help with cooking and household chores. After six months, her CD4 count had risen to 272 (it had fallen below 100). A year into treatment, she now weighs 136 pounds, close to her ideal weight.

Before taking the ARVs, Esther suffered from the stigmatization reported by Ken and nearly all of the people with AIDS whom I interviewed in Zambia. Relatives deserted her, fearing that they might contract HIV from close contact. Friends began to mock her. She recalled, "During my illness, I suffered stigma and discrimination from community members. My relatives never cared for me. People laughed at me — some even do now — and pointed fingers because I was so thin. I have accepted my position and my condition, so I don't care at all, no matter what they say." Esther reported that since her health improved, more than ten acquaintances who once mocked her have confided that they too have tested positive for HIV. They ask her for advice on "living positively" with the virus.

With improved health and destigmatization has come a persistent question that she doggedly asked each CRS and partner staff, even me, "Can you help me find a job?" I asked her what kind of job she wanted. She replied, "Any kind of job! But to go around teaching people about HIV/AIDS, that's what I want."

Esther's question brought me back to the Lazarus Effect. Why did Christ bring Lazarus out of the tomb? To die of malnutrition?

Malaria? To live in a society with 87 percent unemployment? Even as CRS works to save lives, one question pushes all others out of the way: what kind of life awaits a modern Lazarus?

Dorothy Chulu is a person with AIDS whose story illustrates the possibilities and potentialities for CRS beneficiaries in Zambia. Both she and her husband are HIV positive. They have three children from her husband's first marriage. She has been enrolled in the Home-based Care program for five years and has been taking ARVs for one year. Her husband is feeling healthy enough to do all of the household chores and prepare the ground for planting. She feels fit enough to work, but no work is available in the formal economy.

Still, Dorothy manages to earn a small amount of income by selling groundnuts, a staple food in much of Africa, at a nearby roadside stand. The business brings in enough money to buy two pounds of dry porridge, some charcoal for cooking, and a few vegetables every week. She would like to expand the business and its role in supporting the family.

Dorothy appears to be an ideal candidate for the next phase of CRS's work with Zambians living with HIV: "Return to Life." This program, administered through local partners, will address many of the issues raised by healthy Zambians "living positively." For example, CRS is considering developing a microfinance program like the Bancomún discussed in chapter 1. Dorothy might expand her groundnut business with small loans provided by CRS and its partners. Microfinance in as poor a country as Zambia is difficult; the cash economy is small. But Dorothy has already had some success. Access to credit might boost her food security even further.

At this time, "Return to Life" is not yet off the ground. But thousands of Zambians have moved from total disability and imminent death to live a more healthy life, thanks to the ARVs. Obstacles like widespread poverty stymie their development, but women like Dorothy and Esther and men like Ken have indeed stumbled out of the tomb alive and healthy. Whether they will be able to shake off the bindings of poverty remains to be seen. Theirs is the beginning of another story of hope, whose ending has yet to be written.

## But What about the Children?

Another tale whose outcome is yet untold is that of the orphans, who number over 1 million throughout the country. These are the children whose dismal future struck fear in Ken Mwasa's heart immediately after his collapse. The plight of HIV/AIDS orphans in Zambia is one of the most heartrending dimensions of the pandemic. Their life prospects are bleak but beginning to show signs of hope, through new interventions by CRS and its partners.

I met one such orphan, Constance, during an afternoon interview with her mother about the Home-based Care program. Constance is what Zambians call a "single orphan." Her father died of AIDS in 2000. Her mother is HIV positive and takes ARVs. If Constance's mother dies, she will become a "double orphan."

Constance sat glumly next to her mother, offering one-word answers to any questions I offered. "Is it because she is a moody teenager?" I wondered. Later, I learned that she had not eaten all day.

Constance is also infected with HIV. To ask how a fourteen-year-old contracted HIV is to invite oneself into the horrors that HIV/AIDS orphans face. First, there is the possibility that Constance was infected from sexual contact with her father. Second, she may have been molested by an adult acquaintance. Third, she may have committed sexual acts in exchange for money for schoolbooks, school fees, or food. The most unlikely possibility is that she became infected as a result of her own sexual curiosity. Her age rules out the possibility that she was born with HIV. Because of the virus's incubation period, which averages two years in Zambia, Constance was most likely infected when she was twelve, according to CRS program manager Solomon Tesfamarian, an Eritrean who left a high-level United Nations position to work more closely with the poor of Africa.

*Constance, a teenager with HIV, stands outside her home in Zambia's Copper Belt with her two siblings (Zambia). Photo by Solomon Tesfamarian.*

Solomon described how the difficulties that HIV/AIDS orphans face, such as paying school fees, exacerbate the problem of HIV infection:

HIV affects not just the individual, but the *whole family*. If one family member is sick, the entire family puts their energy into that person. They often have to sell off their assets to help that person. They also lose all income from that person, which makes the family more vulnerable. There's no safety net to help people in this situation. They can't afford to send their kids to school. The girls in the family often start selling their bodies to bring in money. This only brings more HIV into the family.

In addition to enumerating the challenges that HIV orphans face, Solomon also outlined the CRS response, a program that serves nine thousand orphans and vulnerable children in Zambia.[4]

One of the main goals of the Orphans and Vulnerable Children program is to confront the root causes of child prostitution. CRS pays school fees, textbooks, and uniforms up-front, and family food security issues are addressed immediately. The educational interventions are essential because, without proper schooling, it is almost certain that the children will remain living in poverty the rest of their lives.

The program also includes psychosocial help provided by a home visitor, as well as extracurricular activities centered on the arts. Health care needs are addressed by linking orphans and vulnerable children with local health care providers and providing training in HIV/AIDS prevention.[5] Provisions for simple renovations of homes have also been made. On the day that we met Constance and her mother, they invited Solomon, Bridgette, and me to travel to their compound to determine if they were eligible for home renovation assistance.

The term "eligible for assistance" did not begin to describe the house. The first problem we noticed was the corrugated metal roof. Most Zambians deal with a leaky roof by slapping a tarp above the hole and placing a few rocks to secure it. This roof looked like a rock garden. Not a patch of aluminum was visible beneath the tapestry of tarps. Inside, the walls of the house showed serious signs of decomposition from both the top down and the bottom up. Patches of bright sunshine peaked through the decay to light a dismal living room, where we sat on uncovered blocks of foam atop a junked sofa.

Solomon looked concerned. The last thing a food-insecure, HIV-positive family needed was their house crashing in on them or standing water in the home. He committed funds for structural renovations, and we departed. During the long ride back to Ndola, he shared how happy he was to have accompanied me for these interviews, because he had found ways to connect many people to new services.

After each interview, Solomon noted some way that programs could be enhanced for participants. Here it was school-fee support for an orphan; there it was nutritional supplements for a person on ARVs. Gradually, I began to realize that this is how Zambians come to fully benefit from CRS efforts. First, they hear on the radio or by word of mouth about a particular program. Then, once a person is enrolled, a home visitor will identify a need for which a different program could help. Finally, they will enroll in the second program and receive the benefit.

Theresa Muleage is one of those home visitors. Several times a week, she visits Robert, an eighth grader, and his younger brother, Thomas, enrolled in the sixth grade. The boys are double orphans, living with their grandmother, who was at the local market at the time of our visit, selling goods for cash. Thanks to the Orphans and Vulnerable Children program, CRS pays the boys' school fees, and they participate in extracurricular activities like fishing expeditions and traditional drumming and dancing after school.

Thankfully, Robert and Thomas are not HIV positive. They are at a fortunate age: old enough to have avoided mother-child transmission and young enough not to have had sexual contact with others. It is an ideal time for prevention education, a vital part of the Orphans and Vulnerable Children program.

Under Theresa's watchful eye, I sat with Robert in a home much like Constance's, but without the structural damage. Rectangular holes in the wall let in the day's last light and the night's first mosquitoes. Robert wore a smart-looking white Oxford shirt, part of his school uniform. As we talked, I forgot about the squalor around us and focused on his intelligent eyes. For a moment, I felt like I was interviewing an intelligent young prospect for an elite prep school.

It took very little time to ascertain that Robert is a young man with dreams. Exceptionally bright, he has picked up on one of Zambia's untapped assets: its abundant wildlife. "We have a lot of animals here," he said, explaining his interest in tourism. Robert would like to work in tourism one day, marketing the country to foreigners like me. What a welcome insight, I thought, after fruitlessly seeking out a restaurant serving Zambian food and hearing only the blandest American pop music in every public venue. Here is a young man who believes that his country has assets that the rest of the world would pay to see! CRS is helping to develop Robert now, so that he can develop Zambia's resources in the future.

## *From Solidarity to Public Policy*

Neither Robert's nor any of the other CRS-Zambia stories of hope would have been possible without PEPFAR (President's Emergency Plan for AIDS Relief) funding from the United States. And PEPFAR would not have become law without the focused legislative advocacy of faith communities. There are times in American life when Catholics, conservative evangelicals, mainline Protestants, and the organized Jewish community all speak with the same voice. When this happens, politicians of both parties listen — very carefully.

CRS's Advocacy Unit, operating out of the organization's headquarters in Baltimore, was at the forefront of the Catholic Church's efforts to dramatically increase U.S. aid to African and Caribbean nations to prevent and treat HIV/AIDS, malaria, and tuberculosis. Coordinating with the U.S. Conference of Catholic Bishops Department of Social Development and World Peace and Office of

Government Liaison, CRS's Advocacy Unit issued "action alerts" to members of its legislative network: ordinary Catholics with an interest in the public policy dimensions of global solidarity. These parish leaders sent postcards to President Bush and members of Congress. In some cases, they visited members of Congress in their legislative offices.

CRS staff also contacted Catholics working for social justice in key congressional districts, like Sister Sheila Kinsey, a Franciscan nun from Wheaton, Illinois. Sister Sheila had been a leader in the Jubilee 2000 movement to cancel the debts of the world's poorest countries. Like many others, she became convinced that without addressing the HIV pandemic, the impact of debt forgiveness in Africa would be minimal. She arranged for Assumption Sister of Nairobi Florence Mulia to travel to the United States to speak about the HIV/AIDS pandemic in Africa. The first stop on her tour: the office of hometown congressman Rep. Henry Hyde (R-IL), then-chair of the powerful House International Relations Committee. Rep. Hyde responded positively to Sister Sheila and Sister Florence's message: find a way to dramatically increase spending for the treatment and prevention of HIV/AIDS.

Work with the executive branch paid off when President Bush announced, in his 2003 State of the Union address, a proposal to increase spending to combat HIV/AIDS by $15 billion over five years. Expenditures would be concentrated on the hardest-hit areas of Africa and the Caribbean. The initiative would be called the President's Emergency Plan for AIDS Relief, or PEPFAR.

Responding to continued urging from Catholics in the Diocese of Joliet and evangelical Christians at Wheaton College (stirred by a timely visit from Bono, lead singer of the rock band U2 and one of the most effective individual advocates for PEPFAR), Rep. Hyde introduced H.R. 1298,[6] the United States Leadership Against HIV/AIDS, Tuberculosis, and Malaria Act of 2003. As a committee chair and a senior member of Congress, Rep. Hyde was considered by CRS to be an ideal chief sponsor for the PEPFAR legislation.

With Rep. Hyde's leadership, the bill passed the House International Relations Committee by a vote of 37 to 8. Before passage, an amendment was added to make some of the funding available to help orphans and vulnerable children affected by HIV/AIDS. Another amendment to reduce the funding levels failed. In the full House, an amendment passed to ensure that organizations like CRS would not be discriminated against on the basis of religious or moral convictions. The House also affirmed an amendment requiring the expenditure of at least 33 percent of HIV/AIDS prevention funds for abstinence-until-marriage programs. On May 1, 2003, the House of Representatives passed H.R. 1298 by a vote of 375 to 41, a rare expression of bipartisanship in an otherwise polarized Congress.

The action then shifted to the Senate, as CRS, the U.S. Conference of Catholic Bishops, and colleague organizations like Bread for the World urged local legislative networks to lobby senators to pass a PEPFAR bill similar to H.R. 1298. The Senate added one amendment, to provide deeper debt relief to highly indebted poor countries, especially those with high rates of HIV/AIDS. The bill passed by voice vote.[7] On May 19, 2003, the Senate sent the bill as amended back to the House for another vote. The House passed the amended bill on May 23, and President Bush signed PEPFAR into law four days later. PEPFAR is now legally known as Public Law No. 108-25.

The passage of PEPFAR was a major legislative success for CRS and its partners, but it was a partial victory. Each year funding for PEPFAR must be appropriated. Congress may decide that unexpected expenses for hurricane relief or the war in Iraq preclude funding for PEPFAR in a given fiscal year.[8] It will take continued advocacy by Catholics and other people of goodwill nationwide, through vehicles like the CRS legislative network, to ensure that the Lazarus Effect continues to occur, so that the lives of Ken, Justin, Dorothy, Esther, Constance, Robert, and others who have been devastated by HIV/AIDS may continue to be healed.

## *For Reflection*

*Let us pray together:*

*God of our weary years,*
*God of our silent tears*
*O Good and gracious God,*
*You are the God of health and wholeness*
*In the plan of your creation,*
*You call us to struggle in our sickness*
*and to cling always to the cross of your son.*
*O God, we are your servants.*

*It is so hard for us to see those whom we love suffer.*
*You know what it is to suffer.*
*Help us to minister in loving care, support, and patience*
*for your people who suffer with HIV and AIDS.*
*Lead us to do whatever it will take*
*to eradicate this illness from the lives of those*
*who are touched by it,*
*both directly and indirectly.*
*Trusting in you and the strength of your Spirit,*
*we pray these things in the name of Jesus.*
*Amen. (Excerpt from Prayer by National African*
*American Catholic HIV/AIDS Task Force. Available at*
*www.usccb.org/saac/prayer.shtml)*

◆ How can U.S. Catholics show greater solidarity with the people served by CRS HIV-AIDS ministries in Zambia?

Please go on-line to *www.storiesofhope.crs.org* for a comprehensive study guide.

# Chapter Three

# A New Awakening

## Organizing Self-Help Groups in India

Sharmila Marandi paused and scanned the crowd seated around her before she answered my first question. I had asked her how life changed when she joined one of CRS-India's fifty thousand women's self-help groups. She glanced at her seven-year-old daughter, Anita, nestled at her feet, and her husband, Premprakash, listening with a few other husbands at the periphery of the crowd of women. Both smiled.

Finally, she responded, speaking with a subdued voice in Santali, the language of India's indigenous Santal people.[1] Sharmila seemed to gain strength as she recounted the changes in her life since she joined a CRS self-help group: "I was brewing liquor at home before I joined the group. Our family was going into alcohol," she recalled. She and Premprakash had built a home distillery to supplement their dollar-a-day income. Although the alcohol produced brought in needed cash to purchase food, medicine, and school supplies, the business provoked unintended consequences.

As the enterprise grew, so did their problems. Both Sharmila and Premprakash drank a good deal of their product, increasingly binging on home brew. He began to beat her following drunken arguments, and their daughter became fearful and withdrawn.

How often, I wondered as Sharmila spoke, do the poor turn to drug production to escape poverty? And is this not the price that the drug trade exacts for its empty promises: addiction, family disintegration, and violence? Despite India's growing economy, widespread poverty affecting a third of the nation's population drives families like Sharmila's to desperate lengths.

Participation in a Catholic Relief Services self-help group sponsored by the Social Development Center of the Diocese of Dumka, India, yielded new hope for Sharmila. Self-help groups build both financial and human assets, employing principles of microfinance (see chapter 1) to demonstrate that even the poorest people can save money, repay small loans, and develop their own businesses.

Until relatively recently, low-income people in developing countries like India could not access financial services such as savings accounts and loans, except for loans obtained through unscrupulous "moneylenders," local loan sharks charging usurious interest rates (as high as 380 percent).[2] In India, CRS works with local partners to provide microfinance services to clusters of twenty women in the same rural village.

The focus on women derives from the same reasoning as Bancomún's — women tend to be poorer than men, and women also default on microfinance loans at a lower rate. CRS-India and its local partners offer training and technical assistance to self-help groups developing small businesses (microenterprises), provide literacy, health, and disaster preparedness training to interested group members, and recruit promoters of new groups. In April 2006 I became acquainted with over twenty such groups, scattered throughout a dozen rural villages in the Dioceses of Dumka and Krishnagar, near Kolkata (Calcutta), India.

In each village, we met with twenty to fifty women like Sharmila, with husbands and children often seated close by. Most women in the self-help groups were married or widowed,[3] between the ages of twenty-five and fifty. The interviews were group conversations, conducted in the public spaces of small villages, with livestock mooing, grunting, and cackling nearby. CRS's development work in the Asian subcontinent takes on a decidedly rural character, as three-fourths of Indians living in poverty dwell in the countryside.

From the start, the meetings took on an unabashedly celebratory tone. After a bumpy ride alongside miles of rice paddies, we entered the first small village. Women wearing beautiful matching saris approached our group of CRS-India staff and partners, placing garlands of flowers around our necks. They led us, singing, to seats of honor, plastic chairs placed before a table set with flowers. They washed our feet and anointed us with buttery oil. The group members sat on the ground, we above them in chairs. They set the scene as if we were important teachers, invited to impart religious wisdom to those assembled. The truth of the matter was that the roles were quite reversed. They were the teachers, we the disciples, as they articulated the profound life-changes that CRS self-help groups had produced in their lives.

### Saying No to the Drug Trade

As Sharmila's alcohol business turned sour, she observed the rising standard of living and confidence of neighbors participating in the first CRS self-help group founded in her village. She watched as each member saved ten rupees (twenty cents) a week, and then noted participants borrowing and repaying small loans from their collected savings to purchase livestock and agricultural aids. She witnessed self-help group members developing small businesses, eventually taking larger loans from private banks to expand those enterprises.

Sharmila joined a second CRS self-help group composed of twenty women, attending workshops at the Social Development Center on group development, record keeping, and basic literacy. At first, she said, it was hard to save money. But women from the original group then showed her how they started: taking a measure of rice from each day's food and setting it apart in a special bag. When the bag filled, they took it to market and exchanged it for rupees. So, in the beginning, Sharmila met the minimum savings requirement by storing up rice.[4] She joined with other group members to cultivate pulses (lentils) and vegetables in a village garden, with the profits going into the group's savings. Sharmila began to borrow and repay small loans from this group savings account for medical care and seeds for her agricultural work.

Then the women developed a novel idea for income generation: brickmaking. With technical assistance from CRS, they verified that the soil in the village was suitable for manufacturing bricks.[5] The group approached a local bank for a 28,000 rupee loan to add to their 5,000 rupee savings to purchase a brick kiln. Impressed by the group's track record of savings and consistent repayment of small loans, bankers approved the loan, the largest in the group's history. Group members purchased the kiln, shaped 57,000 bricks, and baked them to complete the process. Within two months, all of the bricks were sold, for the price of 30,400 rupees, nearly paying for the kiln with one sequence of production. Sharmila's group has produced several rounds of bricks since, fortifying its savings while providing food and medical security for their families.

I could not take my eyes off Anita as her mother recounted the self-help group's effects on family life. She smiled continuously throughout the recitation of events. I found myself transfixed observing the little girl's behavior during the interview as she shuttled between her parents, grinning and laughing. Sharmila continued:

> The new activities are better than brewing alcohol. Alcohol brings in money, but there are also a lot of fights between a husband and a wife when they make liquor because he is drunk and she is drunk. My husband beat me so many times during those days. Now he never beats me. There is a clear difference in our family now: more peace, more joy, more good feeling. I've seen a change in my child's face since we got out of liquor.

I glanced at Premprakash. He seemed to be enjoying the conversation. Afterward, he corroborated the whole story. "Those were bad days," he said. "Everything is better now."

Sharmila and her neighbors named their group Hihiri Pipiri. As the interviews ended and group members served us Indian sweets and tea, Fr. Christu took me aside to explain the reference. "Hihiri Pipiri is the Santal Garden of Eden," he said. "In their creation story, their ancestors came from this place. The term is a symbol for harmony — being together, sharing together, and supporting one another. When you live Hihiri Pipiri, your ancestors will come alive in your own village. So you won't go looking for that particular village; it will be here and now."

Fr. Christu's words reminded me that when I asked Sharmila what she was most proud of, she answered:

> Earlier, if there was a problem, we ran to someone with an open hand, asking for help. Today, we do not do that. We go directly to our group, with full confidence that we'll get help. Secondly, when we have a problem, we get more than material help; we get human resources. This is what I am most proud of.

Hihiri Pipiri, indeed.

### *A Proper House*

We moved on. Often we discovered half the women in a village participating in CRS self-help groups. In one village, *every* woman participated in a group.[6] Wherever we went, we heard similar stories of thrift, human development, and entrepreneurship. In the village of Ghagighi, within the Diocese of Krishnagar, we met Chabbi Ghosh, a member of a self-help group called Freedom, resourced by CRS partner Catholic Charities Krishnagar. Chabbi identified herself as living in two kinds of poverty before joining the group: a material poverty, in which needs for food, medical care, and housing often went unmet, and a poverty of mind and spirit. "I used to sit at home and just ponder and do nothing," she recalled. "Now I am open to new ideas."

Chabbi gained a taste for education by learning how to sign her own name and gaining the right to manage her own documents in the process. That experience raised her commitment to educating her three children. Much of the profits from her growing dairy business now cover educational expenses for the children. She buys milk wholesale, one hundred liters at a time, and converts it to cottage cheese, which she sells to shops in Calcutta. She has successfully grown the family's income to the point that their basic needs are met *and* she saves seventy rupees a month. One of her family's greatest needs was housing. "Before we did not have a proper house," she said. "Now we have a proper house." Curious, I asked her what a proper house was. It seemed a term open to interpretation. "One with a roof," she replied.

Currently, Chabbi has saved over thirteen thousand rupees. With a future loan, she hopes to expand the business to process an additional hundred liters of milk. Her increased prosperity has caught the attention of relatives, who now approach her when they have financial problems. Chabbi does not see this as a burden, but rather enjoys taking a leadership role within her extended family. "Actually," she confided, "the most common thing they want to do after seeing my success is join a group of their own."

Other members of Freedom introduced themselves and described the small businesses they developed after borrowing money from the group and Advance Loans, a nearby bank. Most of the enterprises are dairy-oriented. Some produce butter, some cream, others klakand, a syrupy cheese dessert. One woman buys milk wholesale and divides it into smaller portions for retail sale. She reported (to applause) that she recently expanded the business tenfold with a bank loan. In addition, she added, profits have grown even further since she started adding water to the milk. The group erupted into laughter.

Freedom members are most proud of the group's name. Chabbi offered this explanation, "The group has taught us to experience freedom: freedom from superstition and ignorance, economic freedom, physical freedom, and mental freedom." Those freedoms have been earned through the tight discipline of weekly savings and loan payments and the growing social bonds within the group.

Chabbi and the other Freedom members outlined a typical meeting. They begin each week on the same spot of common ground at the center of the village, seated in a circle so they can see each other's faces. They start with prayers, one each from the Hindu, Muslim, and Christian traditions, reflecting the religious diversity of the group. They sing an inspirational song. Everyone signs in, and they elect a leader for the meeting. The group then discusses any issues relating to repayment of loans and any social problems experienced by group members. They collect both savings and loan payments, recording each transaction carefully. Sometimes this group also takes part in Catholic Charities Krishnagar programs on health, particularly those dealing with the issue of neighbors defecating outdoors, a serious public health problem in this area.

They produce records: meeting notes in Bengali, one of the written languages of India, and ledgers indicating deposits and intragroup loan payments. These records are critically important for gaining bankers' confidence. Loans of up to ten times the group's savings depend on clear, standardized records indicating consistent deposits and timely repayment of loans. Chaina Ghaila, Chabbi's neighbor, produced her bank passbook and proudly posed for our photographer as if she held an award in hand.

The keys to self-help group success are discipline and imagination: discipline to keep timely attendance records and collect savings and loan payments, imagination to develop successful businesses. During a ride between villages, Fr. Christu Das, director of the Social Development Center of the Diocese of Dumka, took time to explain the key dynamics of self-help groups. His passion for human development and love of the Santal people were on vivid display as he talked about the balance between encouragement and challenge that he and his staff must provide. His face alternated between three expressions: intense seriousness, a broad toothy smile, and uncontrolled laughter. He explained the underlying philosophy behind his ministry with self-help groups:

> We have created a system here where the Social Development Center will not give them any monetary help. Even if it's in the area of recruitment, we will not help. They have to find their own source of income. We want to create a way for people to take their own life into their hands, a way for people to get their God-given dignity back. We don't come to pity them; we come to challenge them.

*Chaina Ghaila of the Freedom self-help group shows off her bank passbook (India). Photo by Sunil Lucas.*

Challenge them, he does, but always with a wide smile. Fr. Christu illustrated the point with a story:

> I had a group that approached me and said, "We have saved 4,000 rupees, each contributing 300. So why don't you give us 6,000 more and make it 10,000." I said, "Fine, come tomorrow and I will give you 6,000 rupees, but you must have a discussion before. The discussion is this: each one of you contributed 300. I will contribute 6,000. Now the group becomes whose tomorrow?" Then they started blinking. They came back the next day and said, "We don't want the money."

I asked Fr. Christu if he was familiar with the American concept of "tough love": setting firm limits out of love and concern for another person's development. "Tough love? Tough love. Tough love! Ha-Ha-Ha-Ha-Ha-Ha!" he chortled. Later that day he challenged another group. Several men, husbands of self-help group members, asked for a 5,000 rupee matching grant from CRS and the Social Development Center to purchase a pump set for the village. Fr. Christu responded, "You have just said that you are now liberated from the moneylenders. But you are finding another moneylender in me. If you want me to give you money, I will. Then this village will be mine. Have you already forgotten?" The men grinned and stared at the dirt in front of them. "Tough love!" Fr. Christu whispered to me. The smile never left his face.

Successful groups pride themselves on their fiscal discipline and *thrift*. Self-help group members and CRS staff prefer the word "thrift" over "savings" because it telegraphs the small sacrifices that the poorest people must make to save money. Think of Sharmila Marandi scooping rice meant for the family dinner into a sack for her first savings deposit.

The development of financial skills like thrift tends to release other human resources: business acumen, social networks, leadership. A woman who never dreamed of working as anything other than an agricultural laborer might discover that she is an expert saleswoman, for example. One group adopted the name Hidden Skills after observing this phenomenon at work among its members.

The thrift and discipline of self-help groups has caught the attention of India's private banks. Asit Kumar Paul, senior manager of Advance Loans, is a banker who understands the power and potential of self-help groups. His speckled white hair tousled from a lengthy motorcycle ride, Asit joined Fr. Robin Mondol, director of Catholic Charities Krishnagar, and CRS-India staff at Fr. Mondol's offices for a conversation about the bank's role in providing loans to self-help groups.

When Asit spoke, it was immediately clear that he is neither a social worker nor a clergyman. He explained Advance Loans' interest in self-help groups: "Our concern is to loan our money. We want to loan money because it is the only way that banks make money. We spend money to earn money. We loan out 41 percent of our deposits. If someone makes a one-hundred rupee deposit, we loan forty-one rupees."

Nor is Asit a predatory "moneylender," aiming to exploit the desperation of low-income customers. He offers a special 8.5 percent interest rate on loans to members of CRS/Catholic Charities Krishnagar self-help groups who keep their joint savings accounts at Advance Loans. This rate compares to a 12 percent interest rate for loans to regular customers (and a 36 to 380 percent rate from traditional moneylenders). The difference in interest rates derives not from Asit's love of the poor but from his respect for the repayment rates of self-help groups staffed by CRS and Catholic Charities Krishnagar. These groups have maintained a 99 percent repayment rate, even higher than CRS-India's impressive national average of 95 percent.

Asit sets the ceiling for a self-help group's loans based on their payment records. The ratio of savings to loan begins at 1:1 for groups that have proven they can repay loans from their own assets. That ratio rises to 1:2 with the second loan, 1:3 with the third, and so on, all the way to 1:10, the largest savings-to-loan ratio allowed by the bank. India's National Bank for Agriculture and Rural Development (NABARD) helps to refinance these loans to increase the bank's capacity to loan to low-income people. NABARD also offers training for bankers like Asit to explain how doing business with self-help groups will help their bottom line.

Today, the groups comprise 5 percent of Advance Loans' business. To Asit, the story is in the numbers: the rupees saved, borrowed, and repaid. In total, CRS-India's self-help groups have saved 1,879,786,400 rupees ($9,398,932) in the country's banks. Not bad for the poorest of the poor! Asit expects the number of self-help groups to increase nationwide, but he hopes that eventually their numbers will decrease — not because of their failure, but through their success, as more low-income people move into the middle classes.

Asit located the story of self-help group performance within their financial records. As in Mexico, I found the fuller story of integral development in the names of the groups, which telegraphed the material assets and spiritual aspirations of these women: New Awakening, The Burning Lamp, Hihiri Pipiri, The Rose, Shining Women, Sunflower, and Morning Star. What began as an effort to meet basic needs through the development of financial and human assets has become a phenomenon with astounding unanticipated consequences.

## *A New Awakening*

Before I visited CRS-India, I thought that I understood microfinance. I had watched the tributes to 2006 Nobel Peace Prize winner Muhammed Yunus, read popular newspaper and newsmagazine articles about microfinance, listened to National Public Radio profiles of participants, and received touching direct-mail appeals for donations to various non-profit organizations. It seemed a simple story: low-income people who lacked access to traditional sources of credit developed small businesses when given access to modest lines of credit and "no-minimum" savings accounts. Income from the businesses raised participants' standard of living considerably, often lifting them out of poverty. At least that's what I read and heard.

But when I asked Sharmila and hundreds of other self-help group members, "How is your life different now because of your participation in the groups?" they did not respond, "I was hungry, and now I am satisfied." They replied, "My husband has stopped beating me. He is no longer drunk all of the time. The men in this village now treat the women as partners." I pressed them, "Surely, you have food and medical care that you once lacked!" and they responded, without exception, "Oh yes, we have those things, but what has changed most is how the men treat the women in this village."

These changes did not come easily. In the late 1990s and the first years of the new century, CRS self-help group pioneers encountered obstacles that recurred in every small village. Group founders encountered extreme early opposition from men in the villages, particularly the husbands of group members, regardless of whether the village was Hindu, Muslim, Christian, Santal, or a blend of cultures.

In 2001, when Sushila Murmu agreed to found one of the first self-help groups in the village of Assandani, she did not expect to be accused of witchcraft. Sushila had been active in Social Development Center activities focused on literacy and couples' counseling for several years. When Fr. Christu shared with her the potential benefits of self-help groups, she felt she was hearing the call from God she had been waiting for. Five-foot-four, whisper-thin, and softspoken, she did not appear to be a person who would intimidate the entire male population of a village.

However, as Sushila began to discuss the benefits of joining a self-help group with local women, her male neighbors saw her cross a cultural line. According to Fr. Christu, conventional Indian beliefs hold that men are the ones who sit together and make decisions. Women stay in their homes and attend to domestic chores.

The men of Assandani began to chastise Sushila and threaten her with physical violence. They called her a witch, an action that Fr. Christu described as "a step toward doing anything to her." While the men berated Sushila, a solid majority of the women stood with her, as did her own husband. A few men offered words of quiet encouragement, but never publicly. Husbands forbade their wives from attending self-help group meetings. Nevertheless, the group began meeting, setting aside rice and collecting firewood to generate initial income and savings deposits.

During the first year, Sushila began to see a change in group members. "After awhile we began working for each other for the first time," she recalled. "We said, 'I will work your field.' We attended seminars at the Social Development Center that talked about working together. We experienced three kinds of results: saving time, increasing our productivity, and making our relationships stronger. Through these activities, we escaped the trap of the moneylenders."

Husbands began to take notice of these results. As families reaped the benefits of increased food productivity and income, their opposition melted. "The men have changed," she said. "Even those men who initially opposed the group now say, 'We did not fully understand what you were going to do. Now that we fully understand, you can go ahead." Today, some of the same men who called Sushila a witch help grow rice and pulses on previously uncultivated land in a hunger eradication project organized by the village self-help groups.

Sushila's experience was not unique. At every stop of our tour, women reported initial male opposition, followed by a tempering of views once tangible benefits appeared. In a Muslim village near Krishnagar, group members reported that husbands locked wives out of their homes when they attended a self-help group meeting. The local imam, concerned that Catholic Charities Krishnagar sought to convert Muslims to Christianity, forbade women from entering the mosque if they had attended a group meeting.

Group members responded by organizing a conversation with the imam and leaders among the men. Fr. Robin recounted the exchange:

> The women issued a challenge. They said that they would leave the self-help groups if the men agreed to the following:

1. They would never send their children to the local Catholic school.

2. They would never seek health care at the area's Catholic hospital.

3. They would offer loans to the women at the self-help group interest rate of 8.5 percent.

If these conditions were met, the women would drop out of the self-help groups. Their terms challenged the notion that working with Catholics necessarily fosters conversions to Christianity and singled out benefits that CRS self-help groups offered that no Muslim institution provided.

The husbands met with their imam and agreed to let the women come together without interference. Today, as in Sushila's village, some of the same men are now quite active in supporting the self-help groups, volunteering their labor for group cultivation projects. In another hamlet, we met with self-help group members beneath a beautiful multicolored canopy built by their husbands. They had presented the canopy to the women as a gift of atonement for their early opposition to the groups.

Paku Murmune, one of the husbands, spoke philosophically about the impact of the women's self-help groups on the lives of their husbands, "We men have started helping the women because we realize now that life is made up of both partners. I have no right to drink and fall down in a place; we are to work together. That is the lesson we have learned." Paku said that the men's attitudes changed when they saw the benefits. In his village, husbands convened and asked how they might apply some of the productivity-enhancing principles of the women's groups. They agreed to keep their cattle out of the "second crop," the fruit and grain that remains after harvest because it is unripe, was passed over. Now they conscientiously harvest a second crop to provide additional income for their families.

By the time we completed our tour, my questions about gender relations had become almost ritualistic. In every village I asked

"How did your husbands react to your participation in the group?" The response, in each group, was the same: giggles.

And why not? Social change is not easy. Women like Sharmila, Chabbi, and Sushila found that they were capable of so much more than they ever imagined. They discerned "Hidden Skills." They determined that they could raise their families out of dollar-a-day poverty and discover a whole new set of life's possibilities.

Sabitiri Orang is one such woman, a member of New Awakening. I asked her why the group chose that name. She explained:

> The "new awakening" is that before, I wouldn't even go out anywhere except my house. I used to be very introverted, never speaking up, never going to meet people. After I started attending the self-help group meetings, I learned how to dress properly, write my name, and behave properly according to the common etiquette. We learned that we could take a loan and buy cattle, do farming, or some sort of business. We could save money and live a happy life. In the beginning, I was saving 10 rupees a month. Now I am saving 100 rupees a month. I have saved a total of 3,200 rupees.
>
> I now understand the importance of having a savings account. Before, having a savings account had no meaning, but now I understand that saving money is as important for me as for a rich person living in a city. Now I believe in myself and I am confident with the bank procedures. I am saving for the future, for my children's education. I hope to send them to college.

We can trust that these "new awakenings" are authentic and likely to endure *because* they caused initial discord in the community. If the changes were insignificant, there would be no fuss. The empowerment of so many women at once has created social change, to the extent that, Sushila explained, "earlier, we could not answer men when spoken to; we would hang our head and go away. Today, if they ask a question, we are ready to answer. The marriage used to be a man's affair; now we are partners."

### *Now, I Am Somebody*

When asked about the most important change the self-help groups had brought about in their lives, women spoke first about changes in relations between the sexes, particularly between husbands and wives. Their "New Awakening" also included developing an awareness of the importance of education and literacy. Fr. Christu explained that this is one of the reasons why self-help groups focus on women: mothers quickly make the connection between education and their family's future. "The women are the ones who will educate their children, not the men. The men are always out and drunk," he said, his smile vanishing momentarily. "If the women are educated and develop a taste for education, they will sacrifice and send their children to school."

Chita Hembrum of the Morning Star self-help group is typical of many women who develop this passion for education. She recalled, "When I came into the group, I was ignorant, almost stupid. Now I have learned to write my name. I have learned to reflect. I have also learned how to keep my house and my body clean." Chita is now saving for her children's education. "I want to send them to good schools," she added. Her neighbor, Maharani Murmu of the Milky Flower group, participated in a literacy class sponsored by the Diocese of Dumka Social Development Center. She noted that literacy programs at the Center also cover addition and subtraction. "Now that I have learned a little mathematics, no one can cheat me when I go to the market," she said proudly.

I met so many women who had developed this passion for education that I began to wonder if there was a common "tipping point," a moment at which participants' understanding of the importance of education shifted. A woman in a Muslim village offered an answer. "It's when we learn to sign our names," she said. "We never used to go outside the home because we could not sign our names. For monetary transactions, you need signed documents, so monetary transactions have always been a man's business. Now monetary transactions have become our business too." Under Indian law and custom, the ability to sign one's name confers a host of legal rights. Among these rights includes the right to receive, if qualified, substantial bank loans to expand microenterprise efforts. Once women observe that education increases their ability to act in the world, it boosts their self-esteem and their desire for more learning, for themselves and for family members.

Some, like Mariam Hansdakthong, develop such a passion for education that they become literacy teachers. Mariam, only twenty-two years old when she joined the group, quickly enrolled in literacy teacher training at the Social Development Center. Already literate, she recognized that she had a responsibility to her people. "Without education we will remain secluded; we will be lost in our fears," she said.

After fourteen days of training punctuated by field practica, Mariam became a literacy teacher for the self-help group. The resulting elevation of her status in the village surprised her. "I didn't expect to be *anybody*. Now I am *somebody* because I am a teacher. I have the joy of teaching my own people and the joy of seeing them put their signature on documents," she said. "Other women who were against the self-help groups have been very much taken aback by the literacy program. They say, 'Look at this person, they were a nobody; now they are a somebody. Why don't we also do that?'"

## *We Are Ready Now*

Bani Mandol, a leader in a self-help group in the small village of Chopra near the Indian border with Bangladesh, knows something about the importance of education. She is, after all, a part-time tutor. But she has chosen to focus her energies within the Lotus Flower self-help group on disaster preparedness. It's an understandable commitment. In September 2000 she awoke in the middle of the night to the sound of water gushing into her house. A massive flood eventually brought twelve feet of water into her home. Bani, her husband, and the three children escaped with their lives, but lost all of their possessions and livestock, as well as the year's crop.

Bani observed how self-help group members in the area bounced back from the flood faster than those unaffiliated. The self-help groups in the region provided special recovery loans to their members who lost everything. Bani decided to join Lotus Flower. She was not the only person to join a group after the 2000 flood; in 2001 the number of self-help groups serviced by CRS and Catholic Charities Krishnagar more than tripled, from 229 to 728.

The United Nations noticed, too. UNICEF subsequently organized CRS and other non-governmental organizations (NGOs) operating in the area into a strategy team to help villagers prepare for floods and other natural disasters. Bani Modol became a key leader of that project. Bani now works with Lotus Flower to store dried foods in the highest places in Chopra and teaches villagers to prepare "family survival kits." These kits include a supply of kerosene or diesel, enough rice for fourteen days, and important documents like citizenship papers, ration cards, deeds, and medical papers. Citizenship documents are especially important here on the Bangladesh border, where illegal immigration is common. Bani also instructs villagers in proper storage techniques and the importance of keeping hand pumps away from contaminating floodwaters. In addition, she facilitates assignments of volunteers who take responsibility for caring for pregnant women. Bani, and all of the other women I interviewed, stated that it was the first time they ever prepared for a flood, although they had seen several during their lifetime.

Bani saves fifty rupees a month. She has taken out small loans from Lotus Flower to purchase a few goats and a cow. She has borrowed eight thousand rupees from a local bank to support the road construction business she runs with her husband. Eight thousand rupees covers the rental of a roller that smoothes out newly laid tar. Her husband operates the equipment, and they earn three thousand rupees a month when the weather is dry enough for road construction, about six months out of the year. This sum makes the difference between poverty and a life with dignity. For Bani, floods are an ever-present possibility, but because of her preparation and training, she and her neighbors will not lose everything next time. "We are ready now," she said.

CRS self-help groups in other parts of India have also seen a remarkable return on this investment in flood preparation. After a flood in one community, CRS rushed in, only to be told by self-help groups that they did not need assistance; the food they had stored on high ground was expected to last for the duration of the emergency. The groups recommended that CRS redirect emergency assistance to the "truly needy."

## Public Servants and Peacemakers

The notion that saving small amounts of rice and handfuls of rupees would lead to a revolution in gender relations, a firm commitment to saving for education, and flooded villages turning down disaster aid caught me by surprise. But nothing prepared me for learning that over seven thousand women in CRS self-help groups ran for local political offices during the last three years — and 61 percent (4,334) won election! Many of these women did not, until recently, even know that they had the right to vote. Several are the first women elected to any office in their village.

Most self-help group candidates who run for office vie for a seat on the Panchayat Raj Institution (PRI).[7] The PRI is a local governmental structure, founded by Mahatma Gandhi, based on a Catholic social teaching concept called subsidiarity: the principle that the smallest possible social unit should take responsibility for social life. The PRI ensures a local voice in determining where roads, bridges, wells, schools, and health centers will be built. U.S. readers might understand the PRI as analogous to a U.S. city council, which determines how federal block grants are spent.

On the final day of my visit, I met with two self-help group members elected to the PRI in Bangaljhi, a village near Krishnagar. Having worked as a community organizer with low-income leaders later elected to citywide offices in the United States, I was especially curious about the PRI members elected from CRS self-help groups. What sort of Indian woman living in poverty sought elected office?

What were the campaigns like? How did they determine their top priorities once elected? The two women's answers showed just how similar, yet different, two politicians could be.

The first quality I noticed about Rekha Sadhuka is that she paused more between question and answer than any other self-help group member I spoke with. She stood before me and members of three groups in a red and white sari, matching the dress of the other members of her group. She paused for five seconds after my question, "Why did you run for office?" Then, with quiet confidence, she answered, eyes meeting mine directly. Her glasses, a rarity in this part of India, directed my vision to her temples, which showed the first signs of graying. "It was decided by my neighbors," she said. "They approached me and asked me to run. They had observed my behavior toward others over many years of membership, and saw that I had the most education in the group, a high school education."

Rekha did not choose to become a candidate; the self-help group members picked her, encouraged by Catholic Charities Krishnagar staff to consider running candidates for PRI elections. Rekha selected a political party based on her own leanings, but her self-help group did all of the campaigning. They walked from house to house, introducing her candidacy. On election day, they handled the "get out the vote" operation, making sure that supporters, friends, and family made it to the polls. Rekha was elected in her first foray into politics.

Rekha's highest priority has been medical issues. With no health facilities present in Bangaljhi, medical concerns weigh heavily on the minds of group members. She has worked to raise awareness of government programs providing child immunizations and assistance for pregnant women. She continues to work toward bringing a medical clinic to the village.

Talking to Rekha, it was clear how little her own ego is tied up in politics. For her, it's all about the group, without which, she said, "None of this would be possible." When I asked her if she would ever seek higher office, she maintained the role of the reluctant public servant, "You see, my husband has been quite ill; he can't move around well. So I have lost that mentality, to go further in political life. I'm really trying to give it up," she maintained. Until her self-help group is able to determine a successor, Rekha said she will do everything she can "to make today's mother aware of all the works that she is capable of doing."

Whereas Rekha's public persona was quiet, restrained, and wary of too much public attention, Hasina Banusardar appeared to come from the opposite mold. Boisterous, ambitious, and wearing a unique, multicolored sari, she answered my questions quickly, like a skilled tennis player returning serves. She clearly relished the attention that the public interview afforded and declared herself a candidate for higher office in front of the eighty women assembled.

But Hasina insisted that she was not always so confident. When neighbors approached her about running for a seat on the PRI, she asked, "Why me?" assuming that she was invited simply because she was the best educated in the group. (Hasina was the only college-educated woman whom I met among the self-help group participants.) That changed once she was elected. She found that she had a knack for working with constituents, representing their concerns, and responding to the give-and-take of political compromise. She also discerned a personal mission and purpose. "Now, my primary motivation is to uplift the poor and downtrodden people," she stated.

Whereas Rekha saw access to quality health care as her top priority, Hasina looked at the same issue through the lens of housing. In Krishnagar as much as Dumka, health problems are caused by villagers' defecating outside or in poorly constructed latrines. Rekha has worked to promote awareness of a government scheme to build indoor latrines for villagers who make a modest co-payment of 250 rupees. Copayments may even come from self-help group loans. For those who are already paying a lot for medical care, the resulting decrease in medical expenses helps them repay the loan quickly. Rekha has been instrumental in constructing two of these indoor latrines this year and hopes to help build many more.

After a few successful years in the PRI, Hasina feels that she is ready for more responsibility. She would like to run for president of the local PRI, a not-unthinkable role, as the current president is a woman. Although until recently Indian women were virtually excluded from electoral politics (women with familial ties to male politicians notwithstanding), coalition-building party leaders have treated the women PRI members with respect.

Hasina and Rekha represent not only differing personality types, but also opposing political parties. Their service in the PRI demonstrates that the participation of self-help groups in electoral politics is not confined to one political party. Though their personalities and political leanings starkly contrast, both have found a vehicle to give voice to the poorest people in the world's largest democracy. Their public service is one more dividend to grow from CRS's investments in self-help groups and the women of India.

## Development Is the New Name for Peace

In his seminal 1967 encyclical *On the Development of Peoples,* Pope Paul VI stated that "development is the new name for peace."[8] As in Mexico, it is impossible to separate CRS's investments in economic and human development in India from the work of peacebuilding. The contribution of self-help groups to peacebuilding is manifest in two ways: reducing Hindu-Muslim tensions and lowering incidents of domestic violence and quarreling among neighbors.

In mixed villages, the interaction between Hindus and Muslims is a hallmark of the program. Violence between Hindus and Muslims is a sad feature of India's history.[9] Where possible, self-help groups attempt to build bridges between the two faiths. These linkages grow not out of discussions of religious belief, but rather how group members are to build a common economic destiny. Fighting a common enemy — debilitating poverty — they develop new and lasting bonds. Sanchita Banerjee, CRS-India's state director for West Bengal, has seen Hindu and Muslim women across India come to form new bonds of respect and love in self-help groups. "One Muslim lady told me," she said, " 'When we founded the group, we used to drop the money into a Hindu lady's hand without touching it. Now, look at us, we are sitting hand in hand!' "

In addition to sharing stories of greater Hindu-Muslim cooperation, self-help group participants reported reduced quarreling in villages and fewer disputes over dowries as a consequence of the group's efforts. CRS's own studies of police reports corroborate this perception. The stories of families like Sharmila's overcoming alcohol abuse and family violence offer the human faces behind the statistics as peacebuilding emerged as one more unexpected dividend.

Perhaps the greatest lesson of microfinance is that we should not place an arbitrary cap on the potential positive consequences of these women's self-help groups. It would be a mistake to label such groups as simply "income generation," "disaster preparedness," or "civil society" programs. The possibilities of development are as unlimited as the potential with which God gifted every person, paired with CRS's human and financial resources.

I finally understood this potential while listening to a welcome song performed with interpretive dance by a CRS self-help group in Daharbapur, India. Dressed in dazzling Saris, the women presented a song in Santali, repeating three lines like a Taizé prayer, their hand motions accentuating the melody and words:

> We are the mothers of the world.
> We bring light to our families.
> We bring light to the world.
> *(Repeat seven times)*

Seated before these great teachers, I had a "new awakening" of my own, finally realizing that the potential social impact of microfinance was as unlimited as their love of their families and, indeed, the world.

## *For Reflection*

*The development we speak of here cannot be restricted to economic growth alone. To be authentic, it must be well-rounded; it must foster the development of each person and of the whole person.*
(Paul VI, *On the Development of Peoples*, no. 14)

• How can U.S. Catholics promote the development of "each person and the whole person" as demonstrated by CRS self-help groups in India?

Please go on-line to *www.storiesofhope.crs.org* for a comprehensive study guide.

*Isadro Molinar demonstrates apple-thinning techniques he learned to increase the quality of his crop (Mexico). Photo by Jeffry Odell Korgen.*

*Ludiana holds her son Gaél, for whom the Gaél Bank is named (Mexico). Photo by Jeffry Odell Korgen.*

A school supported by the diocese of Mongu. The area is very poor, with stagnant water and raw sewage dumps. The AIDS percentage is very high in this area (Zambia). Photo by CRS/Margaret Guellich.

Children who have lost one or both of their parents to AIDS attend Adventure Unlimited activities every Saturday run by the Diocese of Mongu and supported by CRS (Zambia). Photo by David Snyder.

Mary Mukaruziga and Jean de Dieu Ntirenganya are members of the
Rossumo Parish Justice and Peace Commission and are also elected Gacaca
Court judges who try cases of genocide committed in 1994 (Rwanda).
Photo by Jeffry Odell Korgen.

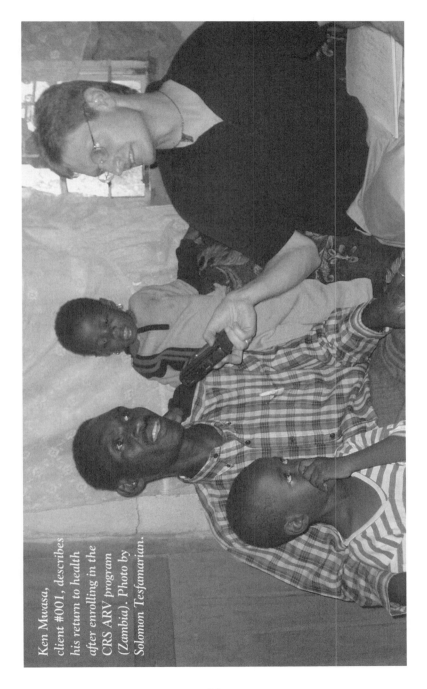

Ken Mwasa, client #001, describes his return to health after enrolling in the CRS ARV program (Zambia). Photo by Solomon Tesfamarian.

*Judith Mumbi, a nurse with HIV, washes the feet of Justin Mubanga, a client with HIV in one of the poorest areas of sub-Saharan Africa (Zambia). Photo by Solomon Tesfamariam.*

*Chabbi Ghosh demonstrates how to make cottage cheese, a microenterprise financed by the Freedom self-help group (India). Photo by Sunil Lucas.*

87

*Most of the self-help group interviews were conducted under a large tree in the center of each village (India). Photo by Sunil Lucas.*

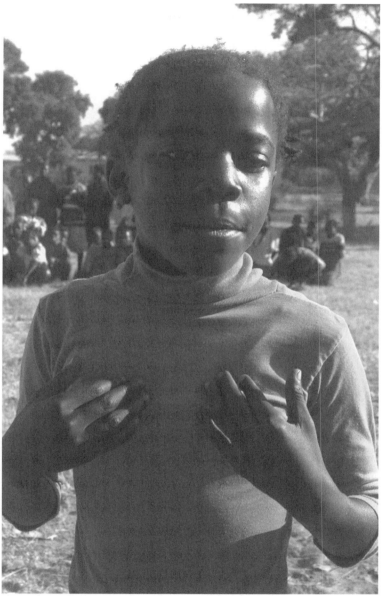

An orphan taking part in the Adventure Unlimited program recites a poem she wrote about the risks of HIV/AIDS. Children can express their fears and hopes through plays and poems (Zambia). Photo by David Snyder.

*The number of orphans caused by the genocide was incalculable, and many young people became responsible for raising their siblings (Rwanda). Photo by Tom Garofalo.*

*Gloriosa Uwimpuhwe (center) translates Drocella Nyirakaromba's recollections of her journey to forgiveness after the extermination of her family (Rwanda). Photo by CRS staff.*

*Thousands of Tutsis were lured into Ntarama Church and slaughtered during the 1994 genocide. The site is now a memorial to the victims. The banner reads: "If you knew yourself, and if you knew who I was, you would not have killed me" (Rwanda). Photo by Jeffry Odell Korgen.*

*Closing ceremony for youth solidarity camp in the Diocese of Kabayi, April 2000 (Rwanda). Photo by Jean Claude Mugenzi.*

*Picking coffee cherries is a task for the family (Nicaragua). Photo by Michelle Frankfurter.*

*Sorting out bad beans (Nicaragua). Photo by Michelle Frankfurter.*

*Dolores Calero prepares guava jelly for use in cakes, a microenterprise that, along with farming organic Fair Trade coffee, increases her economic security (Nicaragua). Photo by Jeffry Odell Korgen.*

*Raúl Cruz, quality control director for CRS's Fair Trade Coffee cooperative, demonstrates the formal "cupping" process (Nicaragua). Photo by Jeffry Odell Korgen.*

A member of CRS-Nicaragua's SECOSEMAC Fair Trade coffee cooperative separates coffee beans from coffee fruit pulp (Nicaragua). Photo by Michelle Frankfurter.

*Engracia Guzman-Cruz shows off a needlepoint project. She will sell the finished product as part of her sewing business (Mexico). Photo by Jeffry Odell Korgen.*

*The neighborhood of Engracia Guzman-Cruz in one of the colonias in Nogales, one of Mexico's most expensive cities. Photo by Jeffrey Odell Korgen.*

## Chapter Four

# Forgiving the Unforgivable

*Peacebuilding in Rwanda*

Just as CRS-India's self-help groups transcend arbitrary limits on their outcomes, CRS-Rwanda's peacebuilding efforts shatter the boundaries we might impose on the potential of forgiveness and reconciliation ministries. But prepare yourself. This story of hope is different from the others in this book, as it is a chronicle of healing after genocide: the systematic extermination of an entire national, racial, political, or ethnic group. It is the journey of a community as broken as the disciples on the road to Emmaus, reaching for the Word of God, the story of CRS working with the Catholic Church in Rwanda to build upon the resources of the Rwandan people, promoting reconciliation and peace after one of the most efficient and brutal mass killings in human history.

On a warm, humid day in March 2006, Innocent Bucyana, Athanase Niyombonye, and Mary Mukanaho sat with me and twelve other parishioners in a circle of benches on the lawn of Ruhuha parish, at the edge of a banana plantation near Kigali, the capital of Rwanda. For over forty years, Innocent, Athanase, and Mary lived peacefully as neighbors, raising bananas, coffee, sorghum, cows, goats, and children. All three are Christians: Mary and Innocent are Catholics, like a majority of the population; Athanase is a Seventh-Day Adventist. There is one difference among the three that meant little in this part of Africa for centuries but became a defining characteristic under the Belgian colonizers: ethnicity.[1] Mary is a Tutsi; Innocent and Athanase are Hutu.

In April 1994 Innocent and Athanase acted on orders from the Rwandan government and local militias to exterminate the nation's Tutsi population. Along with ten other men, they killed Mary's entire family, using machetes and swords, and dumped the bodies in nearby latrines. Mary survived only because she was out of the country, visiting her brother in neighboring Burundi.

The Rwandan genocide continued for over three months, until a small but disciplined Tutsi-led army called the Rwandan Patriotic Front (RPF) captured Kigali in July 1994, and the extremist Hutu government took flight. When it was over, the genocide had claimed the lives of between eight hundred thousand and 1 million Tutsis and moderate Hutus (including five CRS staff) out of a population of 8.1 million Rwandans.

### *Forgiving the Unforgivable*

How do you invite a mother to recall the massacre of her family? For a moment, I sat looking at Mary, Innocent, and Athanase with a frozen expression. Finally, I asked Mary the question uppermost on my mind, "How could you forgive these men who killed your brother, sister, husband, and children?"

Mary took a long breath, as if reviewing the last twelve years. Then she responded:

> It was very difficult to forgive. I had almost gone crazy. I was a fool among other foolish people. The family I belonged to was exterminated. The family I married into was exterminated. I was lucky because I was pregnant. I had gone to Burundi to visit my brother. So I survived with my child, the one I was holding during the genocide. All of my other seven children were killed, along with my husband.
>
> So I was completely discouraged. I said, "Why did I survive? Why did I not die with the others? What am I going to become? I was old; I was lonely. When I would go to the church and the catechist was teaching us, he would read from the scripture and say, "Teach about love." I said, "What's he

*Mary Mukanaho tells the story of her journey to forgiving Athanase Niy-ombonye (seated by Mary) for his participation in the murder of her family (Rwanda). Photo by Jeffry Odell Korgen.*

talking about? He must have killed also, like the others. Why talk to me about love?"

All the people I saw who went up for Holy Communion, when they opened their hands for the Eucharist, I would say, "Oh, poor Christ! That one, that hand, must have killed. And now they are going to have you like that?"

Mary developed sleeping problems. She drank banana beer to lose consciousness at night, but memories of her husband and children chased away sleep. Feeling close to madness, she joined a parish prayer group, the Legion of Mary, at the invitation of Hutu neighbors looking for a Tutsi to join. These neighbors later confided a secret — they had asked her to become part of the group to allay fears that they might be a group of killers.

In 1998, Mary participated in Rwanda's Jubilee Synod, an event which forever changed the Catholic Church in Rwanda. After the genocide, both the church and CRS were as broken as the country itself. For CRS, the horror was both personal and organizational. Five staff had been killed, and the machetes also hacked away the fruits of decades of agricultural and economic development work. The genocide also shook the local church to its core. Some priests and nuns had orchestrated killings. Bishops, priests, and lay catechists had been killed. Local officials had lured Tutsis into churches, saying they would provide sanctuary, only to spring bloody traps. Body counts at these massacre sites sometimes numbered ten thousand or more.

Out of this horror, CRS-Rwanda organized a jubilee commission, in partnership with the Rwandan Bishops' Conference. The commission drew three people from each of Rwanda's nine dioceses, a mixture of Hutus and Tutsis who met regularly to discuss Rwandan history, the genocide, and opportunities for healing. As the commission gathered in 1996, Pope John Paul II issued a call for local churches to make preparations for the Great Jubilee in 2000. Each nation around the world responded differently, depending on the local context. In the United States, for example, Jubilee observances included outreach to lapsed Catholics and legislative advocacy on debt relief for the world's poorest countries.

Rwanda's jubilee commission proposed a Jubilee Synod, to be held from the ground up, in the twenty thousand base communities that comprise the church in Rwanda. Each group of twenty-five families would take up the question of the role of ethnicity in the Rwandan genocide, encouraging truth-telling at all levels of the population. The Jubilee Synod was the beginning of Mary's healing. She recalled:

> When the synod was going on, I wouldn't trust anyone among those who were doing the teaching. I would just attend, but I would not participate. In my insides I was thinking of them all as criminals, except Modeste ["animator"[2] of the base community], because he had come from another place. Modeste encouraged everyone to repent and tell the truth. He mentioned looting, and I had some things which belonged to other people, Hutus who had been in refugee camps after the war.

Mary returned items taken from the homes of Hutu neighbors when they fled the country. She began to speak in the synod meetings about losing her family and the unbearable loneliness she now felt. She found comfort in sharing her experiences with other survivors and Hutus who seemed to regret their conduct during the genocide. Mary began to sleep better and even to care for the Hutus in her base community, "and if I saw a Hutu in my prayer group, before seeing him as a Hutu, I would see him as a brother in Christ."

Then, unexpectedly, Athanase tested that love. Recently released from prison, he appeared at Mary's house and confessed his role in killing her brother, sister, nieces, and nephews in graphic detail. Athanase expressed solemn regrets for his actions and asked for Mary's forgiveness. She forgave him, feeling prepared to do so by the Jubilee Synod process.

Innocent approached her shortly afterward, confessing that he had convinced the others in his patrol group to kill Mary's children:

The man who was in charge of the patrol told me he had Mary's children; he had hidden them. He told me that during the day the children had been in the bush, but at night they came to his home. When we were all together, I said, "Those are the children of snakes! They should be killed!"

The others went to his home and then brought the children to us. Mary was not with them, but another woman was. Along the way, they found a second woman who was part of the family. We attacked all of them with machetes and then threw them into the latrine. Some of them were still alive, eyes open. The leaders ordered us to cover the latrine with soil and we covered it in the morning.

Innocent asked for pardon, and Mary forgave him. More returning refugees and prisoners arrived at her door. Some had looted; some had destroyed her old house, some had killed. She forgave them all.

Since these initial acts of forgiveness, Mary has maintained close ties with those who asked for pardon. She believes reconciliation does not come to completion in the initial act of forgiveness; it is a process. She serves as godmother to a daughter of one of her own children's killers. She encourages her remaining child to play at the home of neighbors who murdered other relatives. Mary hopes her efforts will lead killers to tell the truth about their participation in the genocide and encourage survivors to forgive. She explained:

> I feel like I've become an example for survivors because I live in a housing settlement that was built for those whose houses had been destroyed. My neighbors, whose houses were also destroyed, were laughing at me, saying, "How can you accept to live with those who killed your family, who made you like that!? You would have now eight children or more. You would have your brothers and sisters and husband. But none of them are there. You only have your young child." I said, "Whether you forgive them or not, yours who went

will not come back. But at least you will live in peace if you forgive."

I have even forgiven those who have not come to me for pardon. What I do is to express love to them. I don't say, "I have forgiven you," because they may say, "What did I do? I did nothing wrong," but I live like I have forgiven them.

What is most striking about Mary's testimony is not its uniqueness, but its commonality. As I traveled with CRS-Rwanda staff through two Catholic dioceses, we heard the *same* story in each parish and subparish: Men confessed brutal killings and looting. Women admitted pointing out Tutsis, turning away frightened neighbors seeking refuge, and looting. All reported twice asking for forgiveness: once in public and once in the homes of survivors. Most of those petitioned granted forgiveness.

Behind these stories is a CRS-facilitated process, led by the Catholic Church in Rwanda. Théophile Rwemalika, justice and peace coordinator for the Diocese of Kibungo, explained the work of the diocesan justice and peace commission over a meal of fresh beef kabobs and fried bananas on my first night in Kibungo. As we walked into the diocesan-owned restaurant, I noticed that this athletic-looking thirty-five-year-old walked with a severe limp. His left foot, he explained, was shattered by a gunshot in the attack which killed his entire family of origin. As he limped to the table, I wondered if he thought about genocide with every step.

At dinner, Théophile laid out the post-synodal work of CRS and the local churches. The diocesan synods were the start of reconciliation. Some killers confessed their crimes, but these confessions were only the beginning of the process. In 2001, the Archbishop of Kigali asked the diocesan justice and peace commissions to begin implementing the synod's conclusions, chief among them the necessity of truth-telling, public confession, and requests for forgiveness.[3] Théophile was hired by the Diocese of Kibungo to work with CRS to train church leaders in peacemaking, including diocesan staff, key parish and subparish leaders, and base community animators.

Over the past five years, three thousand leaders have been trained in the diocese and twenty thousand nationwide. CRS invites experts in community trauma healing, conflict management, Catholic social teaching, and human rights from outside Rwanda. These trainers and local educators familiar with the Rwandan judicial system work with diocesan staff and commission members, who then teach parish clergy, staff, and base community leaders. Théophile participated in one of these month-long trainings, which encourage participants to view themselves as neither Hutu nor Tutsi, but Rwandan.

After commission members complete the CRS peacebuilding training, they seek out newly released prisoners to encourage them to confess their crimes and ask forgiveness of survivors.[4] They also lead examinations of conscience within their base communities and encourage neighbors and friends to come clean about their conduct during the genocide. Commission members offer to support those willing to confess by accompanying them to survivors' homes.

The aim of this preparation, Théophile continued, is to reinforce structures of peacemaking at all levels: diocesan, parish, subparish, and base community.[5] The CRS training also enables participants to process their experience of the genocide and appropriate the peacemaking model to their own lives. In addition, the training supports the Rwandan judicial policy of trying ordinary Rwandans who participated in the killings in local *Gacaca* (Ga-CHA-cha) courts aimed at reconciliation, and prosecuting the ringleaders and those who committed sex crimes in its federal courts and at the U.N. genocide tribunal in Arusha, Tanzania. Later in this chapter, we will explore the relationship between CRS's peacebuilding work and the *Gacaca* courts.

Gloriosa Uwimpuhwe, CRS-Rwanda's project manager for solidarity, justice, and partnership, noted the changes she has observed in parish and base community leaders as they internalize the peacemaking training:

> Everyone learns what the other feels. Because someone's husband is in jail for genocide you think, "This is a bad

person." When the woman tells you how badly she feels, how guilty she feels for her husband having been involved, how sad she feels for those who lost theirs, and how responsible she's feeling now that she's learned in the training about people being equal and ethnicity not being a cause for hatred, you as a survivor will understand she's not a bad person; she's a person you can live with.

A genocide survivor herself, Gloriosa has exhorted people in her village to come forward with information about the deaths of her parents and others killed between April and June 1994. She believes that offering forgiveness is not difficult if others are telling the truth and asking for forgiveness sincerely. What makes forgiveness difficult, she explained, is when part or all of the truth is withheld. She, like many Rwandans, is still waiting for her neighbors to volunteer the truth.

## *"You Too Were Like One of Them"*

What does it take to coax a killer to confess a brutal murder and then ask surviving family members for forgiveness? How do people who lost their entire families forgive their executioners? During my visit to Rwanda, dozens of low-income Rwandans told me their stories of reconciliation and hope, fostered by the CRS-facilitated peacebuilding process. Although these stories differed in details, common themes emerged, chief among them the role of the scriptures, or "Word of God," in fostering acts of confession and forgiveness.

Canstance Mukandanga is a woman who did not realize she had sinned. During the Rwandan genocide, traditional sex roles determined the division of labor. Men did the physical work, hacking with machetes, beating with sticks, while women used their social networks to gather intelligence and share information about Tutsis in hiding. Sitting with Mary, Innocent, and Athanase, Canstance described her part in the killing:

On the third day of the genocide I saw one person running away. I said, "This is a Tutsi! He is running away!" The men in the army ran after him and killed him, because of me. After that, I found a man who is Tutsi, and informed the other killers to kill him. Because, we were told, no one is going to survive.

When the RPF came to Ruhuha, we fled to northeastern Rwanda. We continued to inform killers to kill Tutsis. When the RPF arrived, they told us to just go home.[6] When I came home and found the survivors of the genocide, I felt afraid. We couldn't live in peace and harmony because we were frightened of them.

After the RPF victory, the Hutus feared a retaliatory genocide, while the surviving Tutsis were afraid Hutus might still attempt to finish them off.

In this context, CRS-trained lay leaders tried to implement the conclusions of the Jubilee Synod. In 2001, Modeste Mkome-zamihigo, animator of Canstance's base community,[7] invited her to come to the parish peace and justice commission training. She attended and heard Modeste read a surprising message from the prophetic Book of Obadiah: "For the slaughter and violence done to your brother Jacob, shame shall cover you, and you shall be cut off forever. On the day that you stood aside, on the day that strangers carried off his wealth, and foreigners entered his gates and cast lots for Jerusalem, you too were like one of them" (Obad. 10–11). In that moment, Canstance realized she was as much a killer as anyone wielding a machete, by informing on Tutsis and "standing aside" during the genocide. She continued:

> I was like a prisoner in my heart. They told us in our base community how we could reconcile. Because of those teachings and prayers and the way we were being trained, I approached Domina, the man's wife, and asked for pardon. The one who died is not here, so I asked my God for pardon, and the survivors in front of the public. They pardoned me.

Canstance now travels with Domina Nyanzira throughout the archdiocese, encouraging others to tell the truth and forgive. She has been asked to lead prayers in her base community in recognition of her courage.

Forgiving Canstance did not come easily for Domina. With one hand tenderly placed on Canstance's arm, she shared her own journey to forgiveness:

> It is not easy to forgive. It is a very hard and long process. We don't have forgiveness ourselves; it's God who helps us, who enables us to do it. When Canstance came to ask for forgiveness, I wanted revenge. I took a journey from here to Nyamata just to find someone who would help me take revenge. All the way there I was saying, "All the Hutus should die!"
>
> But when I arrived in Nyamata, I didn't find anyone there. That's when I realized that they were all killed. I thought I would find people from my own family, to tell them what happened to me, to tell them about this person who came to my house to confess. How criminal she was and what she had done to me.
>
> I was expecting to find my sister's young children and tell them that problem, but I only found my sister and her husband, who was wounded all over the body. They were not people I could tell my difficulties to, because they were suffering so much. So when I found out all of her children were killed, I started naming every person in our family to see if at least one of them would have a child in the army.
>
> She told me, "You know, when I saw you, I thought you survived. But you've gone crazy. All of those people you are asking me about, come tomorrow morning and I will show you where they are." So we went to Ntarama Church and she said, "They are all here."

The church was full of dead Tutsis, lured to a false sanctuary. The massacre site was left untouched, as it was on the day of the killings, as a memorial to the victims. The trauma of seeing so many thousands of fully clothed skeletons piled high shocked

Domina out of her vengeful brooding.[8] She returned home and began attending meetings of her base community more faithfully. In time, her perspective began to change. She recalled:

> We discussed one lesson from the scripture, "If you forgive others their trespasses, your heavenly Father will also forgive you" (Matt. 6:14). After that lesson, I learned that I also was a sinner. I approached my sister in Christ and I asked her, how did you discover I was a Tutsi? I wanted to know exactly how it happened, what she did, every moment. I don't remember seeing her any single second of the genocide.

Canstance recreated the timeline of the massacre for Domina. She noted when she informed and when the mob attacked. She confided that she discovered Domina was a Tutsi because of a relative's comments.

The knowledge of these details helped Domina achieve some closure about her husband's murder. She added, "I asked her for forgiveness, too, for I wanted revenge." I noticed tears in Canstance's eyes, and I realized these were the first tears that I had seen in Rwanda. Rwandans have shed so many tears over the past decade that retelling these stories did not elicit the emotion that it might have twelve years ago.

Since this moment of forgiveness, Canstance and Domina have become close friends. They participate together in several church groups and visit one another often, sharing home repairs and agricultural work. They travel frequently to rural communities in the archdiocese to encourage others to tell the truth, confess, ask for and offer forgiveness.

Seraphine Ntabareshya is a woman who heard Canstance's story and placed herself inside of it. She eagerly added her own narrative of denial and conscience:

> Canstance helped me. I had committed a sin, but I did not recognize it. I did not take machetes and cut. I pointed out where a person was hiding. It was not a sin, I thought. I did not think it was a crime of genocide.

There was a neighbor of mine who was a Tutsi. He was chased by the militias. I didn't hide him. He hid outside, and then they destroyed his home. The next day, that man came back home. He went to me and said, "Do you know where my wife and kids are so that we can get killed? There is nothing else to do; we're going to die anyway, so I want to know where they are so that we can get killed." I said, "I don't know where they are." I didn't care, so I went to the market to get something.

On my way, I met the killers. Before they even asked me, on my own initiative, I said, "You won't find him very far, he's at his brother's trying to look for his wife and children." So I kept going. Eventually they found him with his children, and they killed them with machetes. At the time, I felt that I didn't do anything wrong, because he was saying, "We're going to be killed anyway."

I found his wife alone in the bushes and brought her home to hide her. We had lived together very well. I told my sons not to do anything to her. I said, "This is our neighbor — don't touch her!" When we came back from exile, I lived as neighbors with her. We lived peacefully as friends because she knew that I had helped her to survive.

Seraphine initiated the nearly completed slaughter of a family, but never saw herself culpable. The father's fatalistic attitude and her generous conduct toward his wife mitigated against any feelings of guilt. Seraphine's attitude changed when she began to listen to the church's teaching on the Rwandan genocide in her base community. As scriptures like Obadiah 10 and Catholic teaching on human rights permeated her conscience, she realized her complicity with the killers, and feelings of guilt set in. Paul's question to the Romans, "How can we who died to sin go on living in it?" (Rom. 6:2) repeated relentlessly in her mind.

Tormented by guilt, Seraphine still never missed a meeting of her base community. She wrestled with her conscience:

The teaching in the group continued. I felt so bad. The priest said that you have to approach your neighbor, the victim, for forgiveness, and also ask God to forgive you. I was so frightened that I wanted to hide. I wanted to keep it as a secret; it was too hard for me. I asked myself, "Should I remain in the crime forever?" The answer was *no.*

After Canstance talked to our base community, I approached the priest. He gave me directions on how I could approach the woman to whom I had committed the crime. He added that if I couldn't go alone, I should go with another sister or brother in Christ. Helped by the Holy Spirit, I went on my own. I went to find that woman and told her everything that I had done against her. All the love that she had been showing me disappeared — all of it. The woman said, I am sorry; I can't forgive you for this. I can't forgive on behalf of those who died.

Seraphine still has not received her neighbor's forgiveness, but she is not without hope. She feels forgiven by God, and periodically repeats her confession and request for forgiveness to the victim's wife. At last she is out of the sin, she believes, even as she awaits the decision of her case in one of the local *Gacaca* courts.

As Seraphine finished, I wondered about the struggle genocide survivors endure when approached by killers. When do you forgive and when do you withhold forgiveness? Is it easier to forgive one murder or ten? Are the numbers inconsequential? We in the United States are awestruck when we hear the stories of Bud Welch, Marietta Jaeger Lane, and other members of Murder Victims' Families for Human Rights.[9] Their opposition to the death penalty seems like an act of Christian heroism, given their loss. But forgiveness on the scale of the Rwandan genocide is even more difficult to understand.

I sat with a similar group of survivors in a makeshift circle on an almost identical set of benches on the previous day in Kirehe parish of the Diocese of Kibungo, adjacent to acres of banana trees and coffee plants. Among the group members was a man whose story suggests that forgiveness is not a question of the number of murders endured but how God works in the human heart.

Justin Ndagijimana was perhaps the friendliest person I met in Rwanda. He was the first in the group to offer a hearty "Muraho!" ("Hello!" in Kinyarwanda) and a firm handshake. But his sunny demeanor was quickly chased away by clouds of grief as he began to answer my questions about the genocide.

Justin had forgiven more people than anyone else I met in Rwanda: eight in all. He had also lost more family members. When I asked how many, he literally could not count the number precisely. He simply said, "I lost my wife, a child, my dad and my mom, my sisters, my niece and my nephews, my uncles and aunts. I can't remember how many; I think it was around sixty-five relatives."

Justin is well aware that far more than the eight people who confessed killed his family and looted his property. But he preferred to discuss the eight forgiven, not those who remain cloaked in anonymity. He explained why he forgave the man sitting across from him, Kanchan Baragata:

> Because Kanchan confessed his crimes, and because the Word of God says the one who doesn't give pardon will not be pardoned, I forgave him. I also felt that it was not his will to kill; it was animal, it was Satan, who pushed him to kill. Since then we've become friends. We meet in the bar and share beer. I gave him pardon, but I do not know what the court will decide. I would like the court to set him free, but I can't control their decision.

Justin conveyed a number of elements of post-genocidal forgiveness in his statement. First, Kanchan confessed his crimes, providing details and the names of his accomplices, elements crucial both to survivors' sense of closure and to bringing other killers to justice. Second, Justin allowed himself to be converted by scripture. When he paraphrased Matthew 6:15, he confessed that he is also a sinner in need of God's forgiveness; how he forgives others on earth affects his own salvation.

Third, he believes Kanchan surrendered his will: to authorities, to the mob of killers, even to Satan. If survivors believe that killers were not architects of the genocide, did not enjoy killing their relatives, and are truly remorseful, it is far easier for them to forgive than if one or more of these conditions is not met.

Finally, he maintains a relationship with the killer. For Justin, and most of the others I met in Rwanda, forgiveness is not a one-time Hollywood moment. To be sure, there are flashes of incredible drama, such as when the words "I forgive you" are first spoken, but a wealth of conversion leads up to the instant of forgiveness, and to be lasting, the reconciliation must be ongoing. Rwandans are the first people in human history to rebuild a nation composed of the perpetrators of genocide and the surviving victims. If Rwanda is to become a country of "Rwandans," rather than "Hutus" and "Tutsis," actions like Justin's sharing a beer with his family's killers are essential elements of nation-building.

## Gacaca: *Justice on the Grass*

Justin's story is also linked to the local *Gacaca* courts and the hundreds of thousands of cases that face these local tribunals. *Gacaca* literally means "justice on the grass." On the trip from Kigali to Ruhuha, driving over pitted dirt roads so treacherous you would swear landmines must have created the potholes, we passed one of these courts in session. High upon one of Rwanda's one thousand hills, the group looked like a class of university students meeting outside on a pleasant day. In fact, they were a *Gacaca* court, led by nine judges elected by communities of two to three hundred adults.

*Gacaca* was the judicial system of precolonial Rwanda. "Persons of great integrity" were elected to administer what usually amounted to a small claims court. Even for criminal offenses, fines and what we now call "restorative justice" were emphasized over imprisonment. Rwanda's new government brought *Gacaca* back in 2004, after the success of a two-year pilot project, in order to try the backlog of eight hundred thousand cases relating to the 1994 genocide. These judges encourage ordinary Rwandans to confess any crimes they might have committed during the genocide and ask pardon of survivors in public. When confessions are not forthcoming, the judges ask neighbors seated on the grass before them to tell what they know: "Where was this person during the genocide?" "Who knows what happened to the home of this man?" "Who killed this young woman's parents?"

Jean de Dieu Ntirenganya is chief justice of the *Gacaca* court in a region of Rusumo, Rwanda. He is also a member of the justice and peace commission of Rusumo parish. After attending a CRS-led training in 2001, he put the church's post-genocidal teachings into practice, encouraging locals returning from abroad to confess their crimes and ask survivors for forgiveness.

During the genocide, local officials and neighbors encouraged Jean de Dieu to join in the killing. He simply shook his head, responding "I can't do this." In most parts of Rwanda, moderate Hutus who refused to take part in the genocide were killed on the spot. Jean de Dieu's popularity with neighbors saved him. When the government held elections for *Gacaca* judges, he was seen as a neutral party, one who refused to take part in the genocide but had no vengeful feelings toward Hutus who had killed.

Jean de Dieu puts his CRS reconciliation and peacebuilding training to good use, as he applies the lessons of community trauma healing and the role of forgiveness to the secular arena. After two years of presiding over *Gacaca* courts, he has witnessed a change in the people: "People are living together, they are sharing, visiting each other. There is progress. I see it in myself, too. I used to see people not in their own image, but in the image of Hutu and Tutsi. Now I see them in their own image."

Throughout Rwanda, hundreds of parish justice and peace commission and base community leaders trained by CRS have become elected judges in these local courts. In Ruhuha parish alone, some 563 judges have been elected from those trained in the peace-building process. Nationwide, CRS-Rwanda staff estimate that

80 percent of judges in the *Gacaca* process are members of a justice and peace commission at the parish level.

One of those judges is Speciose Uwamaliya, a young woman who was just twenty-one years old at the time of the genocide. At first, Speciose resisted becoming involved in the *Gacaca* courts because she thought the process would simply dredge up the traumatic memories of a weary population. Then, in 2004, she joined the justice and peace commission at Ruhuha parish. Upon completing her training, she began encouraging others to repent and seek forgiveness. The results she saw convinced her of the compatability of the *Gacaca* courts and the CRS-facilitated justice and peace commission. As a judge, she now determines sentences for those who have confessed and asked forgiveness. The typical punishment for people who killed, but did not show great enthusiasm or commit sex crimes, is seven years in prison. Sometimes these sentences are commuted to time served, as many of the cases involve recently released inmates. Property crimes are typically dealt with through restitution. If you destroyed a home, you repair it or help build a new one. If you looted household items or livestock, you return them. More heinous crimes are referred to Rwanda's traditional judicial system. Most offenders convicted of sex crimes committed during the genocide are still in prison; no stories of rape figured into these interviews. Many of the genocide's ringleaders are still being tried by the United Nations in nearby Tanzania for crimes against humanity.

Each of the seven parish groups I met with included two to seven elected judges. All of the judges reported that participation in the CRS training and peacebuilding ministries enhanced their standing in the community as reconcilers. This, in turn, contributed to their election as *Gacaca* judges. The judges also noted that the CRS peacebuilding training augmented the government's training for new *Gacaca* judges, which includes topics like the history of *Gacaca,* the various categories of crimes, and the importance of impartiality.

## Challenges to Reconciliation
## and Peacebuilding

Each *Gacaca* judge whom I spoke to expressed hope in the promise of the reconciliation process promoted by the church since 1998 and the *Gacaca* courts since 2004. But the peacebuilding effort has not been without complications. Reconciliation after genocide is uncharted territory for both church and state. At this time, three challenges appear paramount for CRS's peacebuilding efforts: first, complications sometimes develop in the relationship between forgiver and forgiven; second, questions of sincerity sometimes arise about those asking forgiveness; and finally, because some church leaders played leading roles in the genocide, the church's role in reconciliation may be called into question. I discovered an example of the first sort of complication in a base community at Rukomo parish in the Diocese of Kibungo.

Jeanne Mukanizeyimana was an eighteen-year-old newlywed in 1994 when her neighbor, Veadeste Kabagaema, made her a widow. Her story was much like the others told in these groups of killers and survivors. A gang of men appeared at her in-laws' home and killed her husband and his relatives. Years later, Veadeste appeared at her door to confess to the killings and to ask for forgiveness. He spoke in *Gacaca* court soon afterward and reiterated the confession, naming his accomplices. Jeanne declared her forgiveness. The *Gacaca* judges deliberated and they will soon announce a sentence. Jeanne and Veadeste's reconciliation was a success story, or was it?

Jeanne was repeating the story to me when, without warning, she accused Veadeste of not asking for pardon properly. "I have waited for him to come and ask me for pardon, but he hasn't come!" she said. He responded indignantly, "She has forgiven me in front of people!" Jeanne seemed to be revoking her forgiveness. I was confused.

After we completed the round of interviews, CRS's project manager for peace and justice, Joseph Muyango, huddled with Jeanne and Veadeste. Later, as we traveled to the next parish, he related the situation. "Veadeste had not gone to Jeanne's home to con-fess to her family," he explained. "It's an important ritual which requires great courage on the part of the killer." Some killers fear they will be murdered at these confessions. Consequently, justice and peace commission members sometimes accompany killers to confessions, as witnesses and guarantors of safe passage.

Veadeste thought it unnecessary to make one of these home confessions, as the man's entire extended family had been exter-minated. Why should he confess to his victim's *wife's* family and ask for *their* pardon? However, with the relationship threatened by this oversight, Veadeste agreed to reiterate his confession and request forgiveness of Jeanne's family at her home. I arrived at our next set of interviews with an even stronger appreciation of the long-term dimensions of forgiveness and reconciliation ministries.

Drocella Nyirakaromba is another Rwandan whose story under-scores the long-haul aspects of reconciliation and peacemaking. We met her at another subparish of the sprawling Ruhuha parish. During the genocide, Drocella (a single parent) was separated from her children. They stayed at home while she left to do errands in a nearby town. When the genocide began, Drocella returned home as quickly as she could. By the time she arrived, the children were dead. They had fled to their godfather's home when the killing started, hoping that he would protect them. Instead, he gave them up to the killers.

Drocella also lost several extended family members in the geno-cide. However, in the intervening years only one person came forward to confess and ask forgiveness, a man named Philippe.[10] Her journey to forgive started much like the others. She recalled:

> After the genocide, I found myself alone. Everyone around me had died. I said, "Why don't I go back to church and pray so I can live again?" My heart was very dark and broken. The priest encouraged me and others like me to forgive. I said, "I can't go through this business of forgiving because of this man, Philippe. I see him here. He was the first one to work with us in the church, to help the poor, to do all of the church

activities which brought us together. But he was also the first one to kill my people."

So every time they started talking about the synod, I felt like my heart was ready to burst. It was heavy, and I wouldn't get the message. But there was a very dynamic priest here. When he came to my subparish, I would bend my head, because I knew why he came. He was coming to tell us to forgive. After the Mass, the priest would walk around and ask, "Where is she? Where is she? Where is she?" I would say, "Why is he looking for me? I lost all my people; my heart is almost going to burst; what does he want me for?"

The Word of God was very helpful to me. My heart is no longer as heavy as it used to be. I felt relieved, and then I told one of the people who came to teach us, "You know, I think I am going to give up. I think I am going to forgive. I feel ready to forgive."

Drocella forgave Philippe and invited his wife over for a long conversation. Afterward, she returned two water jugs she had taken from their house while they were in exile. The two families shared their story of reconciliation at church, to inspire others to tell the truth and forgive. Philippe helped with occasional handyman work around her house for awhile.

But when the *Gacaca* courts began operating in 2004, a change came over Philippe. He "got tired" and no longer came over to work on the house. He retold his official confession, but omitted the names of his accomplices. He even said in court, "You say you forgave me. Forgiveness is not from you; it is from God and from [President] Kagame."

Drocella was crushed. She thought, "I forgave, but I'm still alone. I will suffer all my life because I lost my children. What's going to happen to me?" Her roof leaked, and every drip of water reinforced her sense of isolation.

One of the parish justice and peace commissioners saw the condition of Drocella's home and offered to help. Commission members reconstructed her house, and the archdiocese contributed the cost of the roof. This response surpassed all of Drocella's expectations and shored up her own healing. Life after the genocide remains a challenge for her, but she is not facing it alone, as she feared. For their part, the CRS-facilitated justice and peace commissions are proving nimble, responding creatively to peacemaking challenges such as this one.

A second challenge concerns the sincerity of confessed killers. Some genocide survivors have said that the church's peacemaking efforts and the *Gacaca* process let the killers off too easily; those who committed genocide are not truly held accountable for their actions. If the killers say the right words, they are rewarded with light sentences and reintegrated into the community.

I felt a moment of sympathy for this view when I asked a killer from Kirehe parish why he beat two little girls to death with a stick. "Bad governance," he replied. It was as if I had inquired why the road from Kigali to Kirehe was in such sorry shape. *Bad governance.* It sounded rehearsed, as if he had learned that certain words, when repeated like an incantation, could unlock a prison door.

The encounter left me wondering about culpability. In a way, everyone we spoke to blamed the former government for the genocide. The government developed the plan; they gave the orders. But where did public obligations end and personal responsibility begin? Didn't German soldiers say "I was just following orders," too? Couldn't they have replied "bad governance" just as glibly?

I shared these questions with CRS's Joseph Muyango, as we continued on the cratered roads to Rukoma parish. With every bump and jostle I thought, "Bad governance." Joseph explained that after training twenty thousand leaders and viewing the fruits of ministries to both killers and survivors, he is convinced that those who abuse the reconciliation process are a small minority. The *Gacaca* courts have added momentum to CRS's peacebuilding work, not corrupted it. He also suggested that the social change occurring is just as beneficial to Rwanda as individual acts of forgiveness. Rwandans, he observed, are beginning to transfer their obedience from individual leaders to the principles of Catholic social teaching, with its stress on peace and human rights. He added that the peacebuilding process also includes careful study of the root causes of the genocide, "so that when you say 'I forgive' or 'I ask forgiveness' it will last for a long time." To my surprise, at the end of the visit, the man in Kirehe was the only person whose sincerity I doubted.

Finally, one of the most troubling aspects of the genocide still shadows CRS's peacebuilding work: the role of some church leaders in the genocide. The simple fact of a Catholic population committing such atrocities is worrisome. But a handful of priests and nuns also participated in the genocide. It is not hard to find stories of heroism among church leaders — clergy who died with their flocks, nuns who hid Tutsis — but it is just as easy to find evidence of church leaders who killed.

Fr. Athanase Seromba's story is inescapable. Fr. Seromba was convicted of genocide and extermination by the United Nations International Criminal Tribunal for Rwanda in December 2006 and is currently serving a fifteen-year sentence. The clergyman encouraged two thousand of his Tutsi parishioners to seek refuge in the church and then ordered a bulldozer to demolish the building. All inside were crushed. The rubble has been left undisturbed as a genocide memorial.

We also cannot ignore the actions of Sisters Gertrude Mukangango and Maria Kizito, two Benedictine nuns convicted by a Belgian court in 2001 for participating in the massacre of over five thousand Tutsis seeking refuge at the Sovu convent in Butare, Rwanda. Sister Gertrude and Sister Maria are currently serving fifteen- and twelve-year sentences, respectively. The two provided fuel to militias who burned some of the refugees alive. They also coaxed victims to come out of hiding where they could be slaughtered out in the open. Sister Gertrude, superior of the convent, ordered Tutsi sisters hiding other Tutsis to produce those hidden in exchange for their own lives.

Other cases against clergy are pending in *Gacaca* courts. Just after the genocide, the stories of clergy and religious complicity in the genocide took a dramatic toll on church membership. Some

Catholics became disillusioned with the church, to the point of leaving. Most of the disaffected became Protestant evangelicals.

Since those dark hours, the church's image has improved somewhat, mostly because of its role in promoting reconciliation. Mass attendance has stabilized. The government has acknowledged the helpful outcomes of the church's reconciliation efforts and views CRS as a major player in the work of reconciliation and peacebuilding. Today, if a priest is accused in *Gacaca* court of participating in the genocide, Mass attendance is unaffected. The church itself is not implicated, even if a clergyman is. Rwandans want those who participated in the genocide held accountable, but the church itself is not seen as an institutional promoter of genocide. Indeed, the situation is far better; the Catholic Church in Rwanda may be nurturing a social miracle, facilitated by CRS.

## *Assets of Hope*

As I sat in the gutted church at Rusumo parish waiting for Fr. Théophile Ingabire and his parishioners to arrive for our conversations, I studied the bare brick walls and empty concrete floor, which awaited a restoration to bring renewal and beauty back to a traumatized congregation. The building seemed to symbolize Rwanda and its people: hollowed out, but offering great promise.

It was a structure with assets, but a building that would remain a hollow shell unless parishioners added their resources. In the same way, Rwanda's Catholics have many gifts to help them overcome the genocide. Among them are a devotion to the church, a love of scripture, and strength of character great enough to survive the worst of national traumas. CRS's peacebuilding efforts build on these human resources and those of the church itself.

Perhaps it would have been easier to fly a few planeloads of international experts into Kigali and fan them out across the country, dispensing words of healing. But this approach would neither promote human development nor foster a legitimate peace. Instead, CRS partnered with the local church, facilitating a process to identify a Rwandan solution to the nation's problem, rooted in scripture and church teaching. CRS delivered experts in peacebuilding and community trauma healing, but the main actors are the twenty thousand laity and clergy trained, who now reach out to nearly every community in the country with a ministry of reconciliation.

Convincing killers to confess and survivors to forgive is difficult work. But it is a ministry that has yielded the improbable: stories of hope and healing over tales of genocide. CRS-Rwanda's staff trust that successful peacebuilding efforts will open the door to confronting other national scourges, such as HIV/AIDS and poverty. As CRS-Rwanda head of programming Laura Dills explained, "You can't move forward on any of those things unless people are at peace with their neighbors and themselves."

I asked Laura what the "tipping point" for peace would be. How many incidents of forgiveness would it take for Rwanda to turn the corner in its collective healing, to own a lasting peace? The country is no longer in a state of war, but the *Catechism of the Catholic Church* defines peace as so much more than the absence of war.[11] She replied that such a tipping point is unclear, perhaps unquantifiable, but she believes the country is about fifteen years away from developing the kind of peace the *Catechism* describes.

Hundreds of thousands of Rwandans have been transformed by the work of the justice and peace commissions, each one offering a story of hope like those of Mary, Canstance, Innocent, and Justin. Many more have grown in respect for the dignity of human life through the ministry of ordinary Rwandans trained by CRS. These justice and peace commissioners, promoting "justice on the grass," have begun to transform the culture of Rwanda into one of truth-telling and forgiveness and offer a witness to the world that the healing power of forgiveness knows no bounds.

### *For Reflection*

*Then Peter came and said to him, "Lord, if another member of the church sins against me, how often should I forgive? As many as seven times?" Jesus said to him, "Not seven times, but, I tell you, seventy-seven times."*          (Matt. 18:21–22)

- Are there limits to what Christians can forgive? What can U.S. Catholics learn about forgiveness and reconciliation from CRS's peace-building ministries in Rwanda?

Please go on-line to *www.storiesofhope.crs.org* for a comprehensive study guide.

# Chapter Five

# The Solidarity Economy

## *Coffee Farming in Nicaragua*

Every cup of coffee has a story. High up in the mountains of Matagalpa, Nicaragua, Oscar Gómez Zamora farms coffee on a little over an acre of land. In 2001, following a worldwide crash of coffee prices, the story inside his cup was one of hunger, disease, and civil discord. During the coffee crisis, small farmers like Oscar sold their crop for a paltry eighteen cents a pound — not enough even to cover the costs of production. Landless farmworkers on large estates fared even worse. Plantation owners halted the money-losing harvest and thousands of farmworkers lost their $1.50-per-day livelihood.

Oscar and his wife watched impotently as hunger took its toll on their eight children. The Zamoras and thousands of other families in the Matagalpan coffee region began to show signs of malnutrition. Mothers fed their young children coffee (the only widely available food) instead of milk to quiet their hunger pangs. Even the most basic medical care became a luxury. Desperate for help, some farmworkers hatched a plan to walk to Managua, the nation's capital, to demand assistance and their own farmland. Oscar resolved to march with the farmworkers and make his own plea for more land.

Five thousand farmworkers, along with a few small land-owning farmers like Oscar, walked twelve miles down a major highway and encamped near the town of Las Tunas — square in the middle of the road, blocking all commerce in and out of Matagalpa. The government summoned riot police and a tense showdown unfolded.

Oscar wondered which would kill him first: hunger, illness, or the riot police.

Fr. Marlon Velázquez Flores watched the situation unfold on television. Interviewed in October 2006 at his current parish assignment south of Matagalpa, Fr. Marlon painted a vivid picture of a crisis spinning out of control:

> One of the first images that I saw on television was that of peasants holding up homemade crosses made out of branches of trees and just begging for a solution to the crisis. My first reaction was fear because the North had been such a conflict zone during the war between the Sandinista government and the Contras.[1] When I saw so many people in the streets and shouting, I was fearful. I was even more fearful when Bishop Brenes called me and told me that I was to represent him in the settlement talks.

Both sides had asked the bishop of Matagalpa, Leopoldo Brenes (now archbishop of Managua) to help mediate the crisis. When they learned that he had accepted the responsibility, Oscar and the farmworkers were elated. The presence of the bishop and his staff would keep negotiators honest, they reasoned, and the church would follow through to ensure that promises were kept. "And," Oscar soberly noted, "if not for the church, we would have been swept away by the riot police."

The farmworkers' faith in the church as mediator was well-placed. Bishop Brenes had emerged as a reconciler and healer during the national disarmament process of the 1990s, inviting civil war combatants to tables of dialogue and adopting the apostolic motto "to be an instrument of reconciliation and peace." Although the situation was tense when Bishop Brenes arrived, representatives of both the government and the farmworkers saw an opportunity to avert violence and work out a solution. Recalling the start of negotiations, Archbishop Brenes said, "When I was present, there weren't harsh words used, to the degree that the chief of police said to me, 'Knowing you were here, I knew that things would go very calmly.' " With negotiations beginning on the right foot, Bishop Brenes returned to Matagalpa, leaving Fr. Marlon, his twenty-six-year-old vicar general, as mediator.

Some people say "the devil is in the details." The Las Tunas negotiations would support this view. Much of the initial goodwill faded as negotiations dragged on and the details of a settlement became a source of acrimony. Fr. Marlon found that producing an agreement both parties could agree to required weeks of all-day meetings, usually extending until 3:00 a.m. Conditions in the encampment deteriorated as heat, hunger, and poor sanitary conditions took their toll. At one point, word reached the negotiators that a child had died, raising tensions further. Fr. Marlon took to fingering his rosary beads under the table and praying for a breakthrough.

A few days after the little girl's death, negotiations reached a turning point. According to Fr. Marlon:

> We were at a meeting and it was past one o'clock in the morning. There was something that came up at the table and there was not agreement. So they began to say very harsh words to each other. I gathered up my courage. I was wearing my cassock, so I figured, "If they are going to kill me, I am going to die looking like a priest."
>
> I scolded the two parties. I said, "What we need to do is put right in front of us, on this table, the people who are outside suffering!" Nobody got up from the table. I was very afraid. They sat down again, and just like children, they were totally quiet. It was a calming moment for us.

Negotiators finalized a solution shortly afterward. The government would relocate farmworkers to arable government land (seized from wealthy plantation owners after the revolution). Small farmers like Oscar would receive help getting legal title to the land they worked (but no additional property). Food aid and improved farm implements would be provided to all by the government. The encampment broke up and everyone returned home.

Today, 60 percent of farmworkers and small farmers eligible for assistance have received their own land. Fr. Marlon and the Diocese of Matagalpa are working with the other 40 percent to ensure that they receive the land to which they are entitled. Catholic Relief Services responded at the time with an emergency work-for-food program and resolved to work with Caritas-Matagalpa (the local equivalent of Catholic Charities) to develop a project to insulate coffee farmers from such abrupt shifts in the market.

*Every cup of coffee has a story.* In 2001, U.S. coffee drinkers had little idea of the tragic stories within their cups. One characteristic of today's global economy is that it obscures from view those who produce what we consume. The most we might ever learn about Nicaraguan coffee is that "the bright flavor is tempered with a round smoothness and ends with a clean finish." We rarely have any concept of the human stories within the cup. Catholic Relief Services is working to change this seemingly inalterable dimension of globalization. In partnership with coffee farmers whose families have cultivated this crop for generations, CRS has founded an agricultural and solidarity project which makes transparent the supply chains of the global economy, while developing the skills and income of small coffee farmers who produce one of the most intriguing new products of the last twenty-five years: organic Fair Trade coffee.

## The Solidarity Economy

For CRS, the key to lifting coffee farmers like Oscar out of poverty and preventing future coffee crises is a vision called "the solidarity economy." Anyone who has ever made the effort to become acquainted with the person who cleans their office, prepares their food, or cuts their grass has already begun to understand this concept. The solidarity economy lifts the veil that obscures the inner workings of the global economy by introducing producers, suppliers, service providers, and consumers to one another through packaging, educational materials, advertising, and even face-to-face visits. These connections then produce positive social and economic consequences. Some development experts, like Alfons Cotera Fretal, suggest that relationships in the solidarity economy become a productive economic factor in and of themselves, interacting with "other factors such as land, capital, work, and technology, to achieve a better performance in efficiency and productivity."[2]

CRS's coffee project provides a clear example of the solidarity economy in action. Coffee is a commodity for which the typical supply chain may include as many as ten actors spread out over several countries. In Nicaragua, CRS collapses the coffee supply chain to bring the U.S. coffee consumer closer to the people who work the fields, pick the beans, and process the coffee. Printed brochures and posters, production simulations on the *crsfairtrade.org* website, and even the text and graphics on the package introduce producer to consumer. For a handful of parish coffee sales coordinators, participating in the solidarity economy might even mean traveling to Nicaragua to meet the farmers, helping out on the farm, and hearing the stories inside their coffee cup by candlelight.

CRS's coffee project began with organizing small farmers like Dolores Calero. Dolores came to cultivate a small plot of land in the town of Siares after being displaced from her mountain farm near Matagalpa in the 1980s by armed combat between the Sandinista army and the Contra resistance. "The war was hard on us," she recalled, sitting on the porch of her simple brick home. Frequent skirmishes on the farm led Dolores to fear that either she, her two daughters, her two sisters, or her young son, Abraham, would be killed. Even if they were not targeted by one side or the other, she believed that eventually a stray bullet might catch one of them. The Caleros evacuated to a smaller plot of land miles away.

It is not unusual to discover women like Dolores running small coffee farms. Nearly half of Nicaraguan coffee farms are headed by women. Where have the men gone? Some husbands desert, some look for work outside the country to wire money home, and some are dead, killed in the civil war. Between a third and a half of the farmers in CRS's coffee project are women.

Dolores described her participation in the coffee project with the excitement of an entrepreneur managing a growing business. At the time of the coffee crisis, Dolores was earning twenty cents a pound from coffee beans produced on her new land. A small producer farming a few acres, she could sell only to the profiteering middlemen who approached at harvest and sold the coffee at a 30 percent markup days later. Getting the attention of a major buyer was impossible.

CRS, partnered with Caritas-Matagalpa, organized Dolores and 230 other families farming small plots of land (mostly one to three acres) into seven cooperatives. Then they reorganized under the larger umbrella of a "second-tier" cooperative called CECOSEMAC (Central de Cooperativas de Servicios Multiples "Aroma de Cafe," that is, the "Coffee Aroma" Association of Multiple Service Cooperatives). Together, the farmers of CECOSEMAC produce fifteen hundred hundred-pound bags of coffee beans annually. Through its sheer volume of production, CECOSEMAC can sell directly to major U.S. importers without intermediaries.

Last year, Dolores sold her crop for ninety-two cents a pound, thanks to CECOSEMAC's selling power and CRS's relationships with buyers. With her profits, she purchased a few acres of land adjacent to her original plot. Some of this land she turned over to Abraham, now nineteen years old. In between computer classes at a college in Matagalpa, he raises basic grains and supervises coffee production for his mother. He maintains that at nineteen he is ready to farm on his own. "I want to improve myself, have my own house, have my own things, and not depend on my mom." And, he added, "I want to help my mom."

Now that CECOSEMAC coffee is both organic and Fair Trade–certified, a process that took three years, Dolores can experience another level of the solidarity economy — selling organic Fair Trade coffee. "Organic" means that the coffee is certified free of chemical fertilizers and pesticides and has not mingled or even been transported with non-organic crops. "Fair Trade" means that roasters have agreed to pay a fixed price to the poorest and most marginalized coffee farmers, a kind of "living wage," unaffected by market fluctuations. The minimum Fair Trade price for CRS coffee is set by the Fair Trade Labeling Organization in Bonn, Germany.[3] Some of Dolores's next harvest will sell at the Fair Trade minimum price of $1.36. A few of CRS's partner roasters, such as Higher Grounds Trading Company (profiled below) will pay even more.

After the next harvest, Dolores plans to purchase a few more acres, so Abraham can grow coffee as well as basic grains on his new farm. Fair Trade coffee will also support Abraham's education — for each hundred pounds of coffee beans sold, buyers will pay five dollars into a cooperative development fund that provides scholarships to the children of coffee growers and underwrites community development projects.

CRS has also encouraged Dolores and other CECOSEMAC farmers to find opportunities to add value to their agricultural products, increasing the cash brought into their farms by manufacturing products that will fetch higher prices. Dolores has done so by selling fruit jellies to her aunt, a well-known baker in the area, who uses the jellies to fill cakes. Excited to show off this microenterprise, she led me back to the kitchen, where a large kettle rested on a hot wood-burning stove. Guava fruits boiled in the pot. Dolores motioned me over to the kettle and suggested a deep inhalation. She would later add sugar to the fruit and sell the jelly produced to her aunt for $98, increasing considerably the value of the fruit and sugar alone. What jelly she has left over, she will hold on to, waiting for a few weeks after the guava harvest for the price to increase. Then she will sell the jelly in small containers to local shops. Like the Mexican apple farmers in chapter 1 (and agricultural producers worldwide), Dolores must use market forces to her own advantage. Part of CRS's work is to help her become aware of when these price fluctuations occur and to make them work to her benefit.

Dolores shooed me out of the kitchen so she could finish making the jelly, encouraging Abraham to offer me a tour of the farm. Physically, Abraham appeared to be about sixteen years old, probably due to some period of malnutrition, but he displayed the knowledge and skills of a seasoned farmer. Abraham learned to take responsibility at an early age, as the only male in the house. Because the family is small (Abraham's sisters are now married), they must hire farmworkers, whom he supervises, for harvesting and processing. Since Dolores joined CECOSEMAC, she has been able to pay farmworkers the equivalent of $2 a day, well above the $1.50 minimum wage. "We get more out of them that way," the young man explained, "and because we are able to get a better price for the coffee, we *ought* to pay them more."

Abraham took me on a tour of coffee production, beginning with a presentation of the coffee plants. A towering canopy of palm trees shaded the dark green coffee bushes. The coffee cherries, now unripe, will be harvested in October and November, when most of the fruit turns red. He will supervise the picking operation to ensure that green cherries are not picked.

Abraham directed me up a small hill to his family's wet-mill facility. Here, the coffee cherries are first dropped into large pools of water. Those that float are defective and will be brushed off like foam. Farmworkers will place the cherries that pass the float test into a depulping machine, which separates the beans from the fruit. The fruit pulp exits and clean water carries the beans and residual pulp (mucilage) to basins below, beginning the fermentation process. The beans sit in fermentation tanks for a period ranging from fourteen to sixteen hours at this altitude, depending upon the temperature. When fermentation is complete, the beans will be washed with clean water. Further sorting removes bad beans, and the wet-mill process will be completed. As we prepared to return to the house, Abraham placed special worms in leftover piles of coffee pulp. The excrement of these worms provides an ideal coffee fertilizer, he explained.

The wet beans will then be dried in screened boxes, with manual rotation ensuring that they dry evenly. Abraham and the farmworkers will collect the beans and transport them to a collection center, where the coffee is inspected and certified free of damage. From there, the coffee goes to the dry mill, where it will be laid out in thin layers for five days while the sun fully dries the beans. Samples will then be taken to quality control experts within CECOSEMAC who ensure that the coffee meets the cooperative's standards of excellence. Dehulling and sorting machines prepare the beans for packaging and warehousing after a final look by human sorters. Abraham monitors each step of the process "until it goes on the boat."[4]

*Every cup of coffee has a story; this cup contains a single mother's dream of launching her only son's farm.* Microenterprises like Dolores's jelly-making business are one way that CRS encourages CECOSEMAC farmers to increase their income. Crop diversification is also encouraged to ensure food security. The cultivation of basic grains, beans, vegetables, and plantains provides additional income. The size of farmers' landholdings eventually becomes an issue for most CECOSEMAC members, however (recall Oscar and his family of ten farming one acre). If a farmer has two acres of land or less, he will quickly reach a point when the only means to increase his family's income is to acquire more land. Purchasing additional acres may not be immediately possible if a farmer is already indebted or otherwise lacks access to credit.

Beekeeping and honey production have emerged as one way out of this quandary. José Escorcia Miranda is a coffee farmer who has taken on this promising secondary crop. José and his family live in a two-room cement block house on a three-acre parcel of land, producing coffee, basic grains, beans, and now honey. We sat outside his home under a corrugated metal roof propped up by two beams, the temperature quite comfortable at this high elevation in the mountains outside Matagalpa. The memory of the morning's ninety-three-degree temperatures and high humidity in Managua made the climate seem all the more pleasant. The house appeared to be the same design as so many others I had seen on this trip: a two-room structure with a metal roof, the bedroom and common space divided by a wall. Children's drawings, newspapers, and Sandinista Party election material covered the wall dividing the two sections of the house.

José explained that when CRS technicians presented him with the option of professional beekeeping, he was intrigued. He had occasionally hunted for bee hives in the wild, arriving home in the evening with a sweet bounty for his wife and two daughters, aged eleven and thirteen. While beekeeping presented new dangers — stings and predatory animals, for example — his farm was small, and four hives would take up very little space. Abundant wildflowers and flowering trees and bushes had sprung up around his and neighbors' coffee plants, the raw materials bees need for pollination. Depending on the flowering of these plants, José will produce up to forty liters of honey, twice a year. He will fetch up to one hundred dollars per crop.

When I asked José what he plans to do with the additional income from coffee and honey, he offered two responses — an immediate plan and a dream. His first action will be paying off $1,500 of debt accumulated over the last five years simply living and working to improve his farm. Second, as his daughters enter their teenage years, the extra income will ensure that they attend quality schools. Between his additional earnings from coffee and honey and the CECOSEMAC scholarships, the girls will also have the opportunity to attend college. "My dream for them is that they will have a better education than their father so they can become professionals," he said.

*Every cup of coffee has a story; this cup contains a father's dream of higher education for his daughters.*

José's, Dolores's, and Abraham's stories are representative of the young CECOSEMAC cooperative. But these small farmers have only begun to reap the benefits of Fair Trade–certification. Their first organic Fair Trade–certified harvest occurred in December 2006. What awaits these resourceful families as they move forward in the solidarity economy? For a look at what may lie ahead for CECOSEMAC farmers, we turn to CRS's strategic ally CECOCAFEN (La Central de Cooperativas Cafetaleras de Norte, that is, the Association of Northern Coffee Cooperativas), a mature Fair Trade–certified coffee cooperative.

Almost fifteen years of operation have helped CECOCAFEN grow into an impressive cooperative composed of twelve hundred farmers. Since 2003, CRS has supported CECOCAFEN with low-interest harvest loans and coffee purchases for the initial shipments of CRS-brand Fair Trade Coffee (while CECOSEMAC awaited certification). In turn, CECOCAFEN has helped CECOSEMAC farmers with technical assistance as well as dry-milling services.

CECOCAFEN farmers in the village of Los Pinos showed our group what the future of the solidarity economy might hold for CECOSEMAC farmers.

Alfredo Rayo and María Elsa Granados live in a small concrete home like José's in the town of Los Pinos. Alfredo and María have lived in two-dollar-a-day poverty for most of their lives, but the solidarity economy has begun to change that. They still live simply, but now with more dignity. They never go hungry. They have divided their two-room house into four rooms. Each of their four children has a university education; two of their daughters hold degrees in computer engineering. Their youngest son now attends college on a CECOCAFEN scholarship, working as a tour guide in his spare time. At one time, Alfredo had to drive a school bus to bring in extra income. Now, thanks to the improved coffee prices, he just works the land. Their three-and-a-half acres of coffee plants, nestled behind a couple of acres of fruit trees and grain, produce thirty hundred-pound bags of unroasted coffee beans.

María told me that she and Alfredo have used the profits from the sale of organic Fair Trade coffee to build a guest house for "eco-tourists," coffee consumers who vacation in Nicaragua to learn about the workings of organic coffee farms while assisting with the chores. In the past, ecotourists stayed inside her home. Now, she and Alfredo have built a two-room structure for these guests, complete with a bathroom and septic tank. "Most foreigners are afraid to sit on latrines," she confided. "We had to build the bathroom for them. But it was a dream come true for me because I like bathrooms too!"

María and Alfredo earn $4.50 a day from ecotourists, plus $2.30 for each meal they prepare. Ecotourism provides an additional stream of income, particularly at harvest time, but it also serves as an important link in the solidarity economy. Coffee consumers who visit their farm are never the same; a week on the farm produces lasting bonds of solidarity. When these ecotourists purchase a package of CECOCAFEN coffee back in the United States, they remember María and Alfredo, who represent the twelve hundred families in CECOCAFEN in a way no cartoon logo on a coffee package ever could.[5]

As María and her neighbors in CECOCAFEN move out of poverty, their dreams for the village of Los Pinos grow. Now that she, her family, and others in the community have food security, they desire greater access to health care:

> Here in our community, the nearest health center is over four miles away. We can't always get the health services we need. Even if you go to a hospital, they'll see you, but they can't give you the medicine you need. The people who have less resources will walk four miles and then are told that they don't have any medicine. So kids, pregnant women, and mothers die.

María believes that Fair Trade coffee and ecotourism might help provide the capital to build a health center, and, with the concentrated population of Los Pinos, such an operation could sustain itself. It's a belief, she said, that is spreading throughout Los Pinos.

*Every cup of coffee has a story; this cup contains a village's dream of decent health care for all of its residents.*

Nicaragua's civil war was trying for María and most other coffee farmers in the Matagalpan region. On the one hand she was elated by the results. "The dictatorship was gone!" she said proudly. But the war between the Contra resistance and the Sandinista government took a heavy toll on her family. Her brothers and male cousins were drafted into the national army. Even when they survived combat, their military service was noted by Contra sympathizers. "Our family was afraid that when a boy came back, the Contras would kill him," she recalled, her eyes filling with tears. "Half of my family was killed because they fulfilled their military service."

But today, María has no difficulty working with former Contras in CECOCAFEN, whose membership appeared to be equally divided between the two former combatants and their sympathizers. "The war is over. What happened, happened," she said with resignation. "We have to forget about the war. Now everyone needs to get back to work." That war-weary attitude was everywhere I went in Nicaragua. Whether former Contra or former Sandinista, the coffee farmers of CECOSEMAC consistently echoed María's sentiments.

Yet most of the twenty-five CECOSEMAC farmers with whom I spoke were evasive about their own involvement in the war. A well-known Sandinista army veteran claimed that he had secured a draft deferment while caring for his maiden aunts during the war. A gun-runner for the Contras caught delivering twenty weapons to fighters in the mountains said that he was arrested and his truck seized "for no reason." But they all repeated the sentiments of coffee farmer and beekeeper José, who lost two entire branches of his family tree in the fighting. José told me, "What we had here was an armed conflict among brothers. We're not going to base our actions today on the weaknesses that were present at that time. Nowadays we don't see the differences. We live together; we work together as a cooperative; and we are all aspiring for the well-being of our community."

Many of the Nicaraguans whom I interviewed credited former president Violeta Chamorro with winning the population over to peace. "Violeta said, 'I have two sons who were Sandinista and two who were Contra. We've got to learn to live together and eat at the same table,'" one interviewee paraphrased. Many also praised Archbishop Brenes for successfully applying his motto, "to be an instrument of reconciliation and peace," through the convening of reconciliation dialogues throughout the diocese. When asked about relations among the former combatants today, Archbishop Brenes concluded, "I believe that the people don't want war. Because all of them have suffered. All of them have lost some family member, and the wounds are quite deep. They don't want those wounds to come back."

*Every cup of coffee has a story. This cup contains a people's prayer for peace.*

CECOSEMAC and CECOCAFEN provide arenas through which coffee farmers take on the common challenge of poverty while healing the wounds of a devastating civil war. Dolores, Abraham, María, and Alfredo stand at the forefront of new strategies to lift low-income farmers out of poverty while building a society of reconciliation. But these efforts will succeed only if coffee farmers continue to increase the quality of their coffee for the North American premium coffee market. That attention to quality control begins on the farm but is honed in the laboratories of Caritas-Matagalpa.

### *A Cup of Excellence*

Raúl Cruz slid the drawer of his laboratory coffee roaster open and studied the color of the carefully measured 150 gram sample. "Too light," he said, closing the drawer for a second to continue roasting, opening it and then closing it again for another second. He repeated the process three times. "Just right! Not too dark!" he announced, opening the drawer and emptying the roasted beans into a ventilator for cooling.

Raúl is a professional coffee taster and director of quality control for CECOSEMAC. The twenty-six-year-old son of an organic Fair Trade coffee farmer, Raúl rates samples from CECOSEMAC farmers and investigates potential problems when the samples do not measure up to expected quality. He got started as a teenager, tasting coffee on his father's farm and rating it for quality. After he completed taster's training in his father's coffee cooperative, he traveled to the United States for advanced courses. Raúl is now recognized as one of the premiere coffee tasters in Nicaragua. Displayed on the laboratory wall is a plaque noting his service as a judge for the 2006 Cup of Excellence festival, a prestigious international competition.

Setting up four glass cups of equal size on the laboratory counter, Raúl demonstrated the work of a taster — the formal "cupping" process. After grinding the cooled beans, he measured a tablespoon of coffee for each cup. Then he poured enough boiling water to cover the fragrant coffee. But the smell that I savored was not sufficient for Raúl. He evaluated the look of the coffee crust and lowered his head, nostrils level with the top of the cup. Breaking the crust with a spoon, he inhaled deeply. After rating the crust and its aroma, Raúl took a large spoonful of coffee and sipped, evoking a shrill whistle.

He swished the coffee around his mouth, spat it into the sink, and returned to his clipboard, ranking the coffee along an 8-point scale in such categories as aroma, sweetness, acidity, mouth feel, flavor, aftertaste, and the balance of flavors. He totaled the scores. This sample rated 88.5 on the hundred-point scale, right where it should be. Raúl explained that Nicaraguan organic coffee for the Fair Trade market should score between 85 and 90. Only specialty coffees for high-end markets break into the 90 to 100 range. A score below 85 indicates a problem with the production process.

Tasters are important to coffee production because a skilled cupper can discern specific problems and recommend solutions to the farmer. If Raúl tastes a defect in a coffee sample, he visits the farm to inspect each step of production. "When you find coffee that has a certain flavor, you know that they are picking too much of the unripe coffee beans," he explained. "If I taste a problem with the fermentation, I'll know that there is a problem with the wet milling, when they are laying it out. If it tastes moldy, I'll know there is a problem with the packaging process."

Raúl explained that while he appraises a good deal of the coffee produced by CECOSEMAC, one of the most important parts of his job is training the teenage children of farmers. Young adults make good tasters because their sense of taste is strong. They are also keenly aware of the relationship between quality coffee and family well-being. Raúl's aim is to have an apprentice taster in each of CECOSEMAC's two hundred family farms. With his training, a farmer's son or daughter might provide feedback that could produce the next Cup of Excellence winner.

I asked Raúl what coffee *he* drinks when he is not "cupping." He replied that he favors organic coffee from his father's farm. Curious, I asked if he would one day take over the family farm. Unexpectedly, his eyes welled up. "Maybe," he said. For the first time, I wondered if new career choices would place a strain on coffee-producing families, as farmers provide more education for their children and professional occupations open up. Children who attend universities and develop an interest in computers may not want to return to the family farm. We know this story all too well in the United States. For now, Raúl has charted a middle path, working inside a coffee cooperative as a professional.

CRS promotes the quality control efforts of Nicaraguans like Raúl but also brings in the resources of other U.S. Catholic organizations. Professor Sue Jackels of Seattle University, a Jesuit institution, is a chemist who answered a specific call to solidarity. Sue had attended meetings of a worldwide association of chemists from Jesuit universities (ISJACHEM) for several years. In 2001, a colleague from the University of Central America (UCA)–Nicaragua stood up in a plenary session and encouraged members of the organization to help lead a response to the coffee crisis:

> He said, "As chemists, there is something we can do about it."
> I heard that and I thought, "I don't know what it is that I can do. I just can't wrap my brain around that idea." But I started reading. So the next year he got up and said that nobody had responded. He said, "If we don't do something about this, I am going to stop coming to these meetings." So I got up and said, "Okay, I am going to figure out something to do. I'm going to consider something, some way to get involved." So I started reading more and talking to people on campus.

Sue spoke to Janet Quillian, director of Seattle University's International Development Internship Program and learned of CRS's coffee project. She initiated a conversation with CRS-Nicaragua staff to determine how she might help.

CRS staff reported fears that the fermentation process was going awry for a significant number of CECOSEMAC farmers. "The concern was that the farmers were just letting the fruit mucilage ferment too long, and this was degrading the coffee quality," she explained. After studying the problem, Sue came to believe that an experiment measuring the changing acidity of the mucilage might help the farmers understand what was going wrong.

She and her husband, Charles, a chemist at the University of Washington–Bothell, applied for research sabbaticals to study the fermentation process in CECOSEMAC farms. In 2004, they traveled to Nicaragua with two of Sue's students, joining up with a University of Central America (UCA)–Nicaragua student to form a research team. They devised and carried out an experiment in response to the *farmers'* research questions, a scientific application of the preferential option for the poor. The small coffee plots became the Jackels' laboratory; the farmers became amateur chemists.

Sue and her team distributed pH strips to participating farmers, who measured the pH of three coffee samples at regular intervals during fermentation. They halted the process by washing the beans when the pH decreased to 4.6, 4.3, and 3.9 for the three samples. Lower pH indicated higher acidity.

Anyone who has baked a cake "until a toothpick comes out clean" will understand the late stages of coffee fermentation. If a farmer pokes the fermenting mucilage with a stick early in the process, the hole made by the stick fills in quickly. If she does so when the process is completed, the hole persists, and the beans rub against each other with more friction. If the farmer does not wash the beans soon enough, the fermentation continues, the coffee becomes too acidic, and taste quality is compromised (recall Raúl's acidity scale).

The research team gathered the coffee samples and then dried and roasted the beans. Raúl's CECOSEMAC laboratory and CECOCAFEN's quality control department then evaluated the various samples through a formal cupping process. The results indicated a correlation between the pH of the coffee at washing and the quality of the roasted coffee — the longer the fermentation, the more acidic the coffee, with an accompanying decline in taste quality.[6] Farmers then refined their practice of the traditional fermentation process based on the results. Their test for "doneness" remained the same — when a hole made by a stick persisted — but they gained valuable quantitative data that encouraged them to more carefully monitor the process and accurately gauge its completion.

*Pedro Ortiz is the CRS coffee farmer whose photograph can be found on many bags of CRS Fair Trade Coffee (Nicaragua). Photo by Michelle Frankfurter.*

One reason this quality control project worked was that the CECOSEMAC farmers took their own pH measurements and recorded their own observations, increasing their own skill-set in the process. Charles was especially impressed with the farmers as researchers and adult learners:

> These folks generally don't have a large education base to build on. Many of them quit school at sixth grade. But they're superb adult learners. When you go on the farm and talk to them, they show great attention to detail. They take good notes about what they are doing, they are very careful, and they report back afterward. They are extremely easy to work with, and they learn very rapidly. They are the kind of adult learners that we look for in our university students.
>
> The farmers are keenly aware of the role of technology and education in being keys to improving their process. They also have a very long-term view, which interested me. I didn't expect this. When you talk to them about coffee, they're not simply asking, "How will this help me next year?" They are asking, "Will this help me develop a method of farming and an approach that will have sustainability over the long run?"

Charles believes that coffee farmers develop this long-term view because coffee is a crop that requires years of investment. Four years of cultivation after planting are required before a decent yield results. With proper care, the trees can produce viable crops for fifteen to thirty years. But reliance on income from coffee production can be a risky proposition, considering historically wide market fluctuations, without elements of the solidarity economy such as cooperative membership, Fair Trade–certification, and technical assistance provided through CRS and scientists like Sue and Charles.

Sue noted that Seattle University has also sent engineers, economists, nurses, and law school professors down to Nicaragua. Twenty years ago, students who wished to show solidarity with Nicaraguans might travel to help with the coffee harvest. Now young adults bring their budding professional skills to bear in true service-learning projects. Civil engineering students build school cafeterias; nursing students provide health care; and Sue's students study the chemistry of coffee while helping low-income farmers produce a "cup of excellence." CRS has helped to usher in this new era of service-learning by respecting both the skills of low-income coffee farmers and the resources university students and their professors have to offer.

*Every cup of coffee has a story. This "cup of excellence" is brought to you by CECOSEMAC quality control experts working in solidarity with U.S. chemists.*

### Reaching for Higher Grounds

Quality control efforts are important, but without buyers CRS's coffee project would not lift small farmers out of poverty. It's a sad fact of the coffee market that 80 percent of the Fair Trade–certified coffee in the world is sold on conventional terms because of a shortage of Fair Trade buyers. For this reason, the success of CRS's coffee project depends on generating new markets in the United States for Fair Trade coffee. Of equal importance is developing strong relationships with coffee roasters in the United States. These roasters complete the coffee production process and market to U.S. consumers. CRS partner roasters in the United States are a special breed, a group of business people who seek out the untested farmer, the small producer, the poorest of the poor, to pay them what might be the first fair price they ever received for a hundred-pound bag of coffee beans.

Chris Treter is one such roaster. Chris never expected to become a Fair Trade coffee importer, but he is now a key CRS partner. The roots of the Michigan coffee roaster's concern for Latin American farmers go back to his Toledo, Ohio, high school experience. When Chris arrived for class at St. John's Jesuit High School on the morning of November 17, 1989, the problems of El Salvador were the furthest thing from his mind. But the somber tone on campus communicated to him that something was wrong. He learned from classmates that six Jesuits, their housekeeper, and her daughter had been murdered the previous night by elements of the Salvadoran military. "Classes were canceled for the day and everyone went into the chapel for prayer," he recalled. "They told us what happened. I had no idea even where El Salvador was or what was going on. That experience made it more familiar to me. It helped open doors at the time and then helped me to ask questions later in life."

The shock (and teaching) of that day left an indelible imprint on Chris. His pastor's homilies about "one human family" began to make sense. He discovered a world beyond Toledo through study and travel. Chris grew more familiar with Latin America and Catholic social teaching in the 1990s, working with the children of migrants from Central America and other parts of Mexico in Tijuana, Mexico. There, he met his future wife, Jody, a fellow Midwesterner. After they married and moved to Chiapas, Mexico, Chris and Jody brainstormed an idea to help the low-income farmers they had come to know — a Fair Trade coffee importing business called Higher Grounds Trading Company. "The non-profits we had been working with were unable to deliver on their mission because of their constant need to raise money," Chris explained. A development organization with secure funding built-in might fare better, they reasoned.

Four years later, Higher Grounds is a $500,000 company and growing at a rate of 60 percent a year. Its mission is to help some of the poorest farmers in Latin America receive a fair price for the premium coffee that they produce. Higher Grounds currently pays nine cents more than the minimum Fair Trade price of $1.36. Within their importing cooperative, Cooperative Coffees (an organization of small roasters), Chris and Jody push for even higher prices. In 2007, roasters affiliated with Cooperative Coffees (including all of CRS's partner roasters) will purchase coffee at nineteen cents above the Fair Trade minimum price.

At first, creditors refused to invest in this business model. "Bankers thought we were naive to pay so much for coffee and then to help with development projects like installing a water system in a Mayan community in Chiapas," Chris explained. Over time, sales figures won over loan officers at CitiBank, who recently approved a loan to update and upgrade Higher Grounds' roasting equipment.

Local Catholic customers were also slow to warm to Fair Trade coffee. Higher Grounds is located within the Diocese of Gaylord, Michigan, which partners with the Diocese of Matagalpa through CRS (see below).The coffee beans that CECOSEMAC sells to Higher Grounds are grown in the Diocese of Matagalpa. But Chris received a cool reception when he pitched Matagalpan coffee to parishes in the Gaylord diocese. "I didn't do a very good job of laying it out to them," he said. "People were a little skeptical that a business person would sell them something because it's a good thing and not just trying to make money."

That skepticism turned around after a delegation of priests and laypeople from the Diocese of Matagalpa visited Gaylord in May 2006. When parishioners asked, "How can we help?" one of the Nicaraguan priests responded, "Enjoy our coffee." Sales to Catholic parishes and Gaylord's Catholic Center quickly jumped from zero to 250 pounds a month, where they have now stabilized. Chris has no doubt that the CRS-brokered diocesan partnership brought about this change. "I attribute it all to the diocese showing the face behind the coffee," he said.

In addition to church sales, Higher Grounds markets to restaurants, coffee houses, food co-ops, and specialty stores. Sales to big chains, though lucrative, are not in the Higher Grounds business model. You will not find Higher Grounds roasted coffee in Wal-Mart.[7] Their company's aim, Chris described, is to stay within a solidarity economy model of small farmers selling to small roasters selling to small retailers. At the end of a long day running a fast-growing business, these are the higher grounds that Chris and Jody occupy.

*Every cup of coffee has a story. This cup is brought to you by CRS partner roasters who translate idealism into action by marketing organic Fair Trade coffee to U.S. consumers.*

## Solidarity in Action

One need not be a coffee roaster, chemist, or even a coffee drinker to live in solidarity with CECOSEMAC farmers. For some Catholics, it may be a matter as simple as participating in Operation Rice Bowl (*orb.crs.org*). In 2006, CRS's Lenten Pray-Fast-Learn-Give program shone a spotlight on CRS-Nicaragua's coffee project. Education materials profiled farmers like María Antonia Blandón Guillén, who earned 18 cents a pound for her coffee in 2001 and now makes $1.36 a pound through CECOSEMAC. Internet links refer readers to a virtual coffee tour at *fairtrade.crs.org*.

A simulation game in the Operation Rice Bowl *Educator's Guide* helps children relate to the concept of Fair Trade. Grade school students pretend that they are selling jewelry to support their families. They purchase supplies, manufacture necklaces, and sell the completed jewelry. They pay ten cents for beads, and five cents for string. When the necklace is completed, the buyer insists on paying ten cents for the whole necklace. The jewelers have to sell at the unfair price; otherwise they are simply stuck with a necklace. Then, in the final stage of the simulation, all of the jewelers come together in a cooperative to set a "fair price" and repeat the buying activity. Older children utilize resources in the *Educator's Guide* to research the availability of Fair Trade coffee locally and write to local retailers to encourage the sale of Fair Trade coffee.

Operation Rice Bowl is foremost an education program, but it also includes an almsgiving component. Those alms add up. In 2006, CRS collected $7.4 million. CRS distributed $5.4 million to food security and agricultural development programs in forty-five countries and returned $2 million to U.S. dioceses to fund local hunger programs. CRS awarded $50,000 of the 2006 collection to the Coffee Solidarity Marketing Program, led by Michigan State University's Partnership for Food Industry Development.

In addition to participating in Operation Rice Bowl, Catholics in the Diocese of Gaylord, Michigan, have taken advantage of a special opportunity to live in solidarity with their counterparts in the coffee-growing region of Matagalpa, Nicaragua. The two dioceses partner via a CRS-brokered relationship to share faith, culture, and resources. "The great thing about it," said Diocese of Gaylord partnership chair Nita Send of St. Michael the Archangel parish, "is that it was set up as a lasting partnership. It wasn't like a group of us were going to go down and paint some houses and then come back home. It's a long-term relationship where we learn from each other."

Fr. Walt Derylo of the Diocese of Gaylord traces the beginnings of the partnership to Pope John Paul II's 1999 statement *The Church in America*, in which the pope urged Catholics in North, South, and Central America to view themselves as one church, one America. Fr. Derylo credits Bishop Patrick Cooney with developing the vision to bring the two dioceses together through CRS:

> Our bishop recognizes that we live — even in our basic rural diocese here — in something of an American cocoon. We're not always aware of realities in other parts of the world, especially with regard to social justice. Going into a relationship with people in another part of the world through our faith connection, that is really transformative. And that is the ultimate goal, a transformation of our own perspective on this planet, why we're here together, how that's part of the divine plan, and how we can live out a relationship of solidarity.

In 2004, when the partnership was officially launched, Bishop Cooney visited then-Bishop Brenes in the Diocese of Matagalpa.

Two delegations of Nicaraguans have now visited Gaylord, and two Gaylord delegations have traveled to Nicaragua. Various spin-off ministries have developed, such as selling CECOSEMAC coffee in Michigan parishes, improving rural chapels in Nicaragua, and funding Nicaraguan radio evangelization. Future plans include a medical mission and school-to-school partnerships.

The most striking aspect of the partnership is the development of face-to-face relationships. Fr. Derylo believes that this experience is the heart of what it means to be in partnership:

Solidarity happens when you get to know each other, and you begin to share your faith and your relationships with each other. There's no substitute for real human stories. Jesus did not write a catechism; he just told stories. And we're still telling those same stories today because they're so alive. So these stories of our experience in Nicaragua and the people that we have met and come to know and love — this is what makes the connection. Once you know someone, they're not blank faces or words in a political sound bite.

Nita was one Gaylord parishioner profoundly affected by meeting the Matagalpans face-to-face:

With all our good intentions, we still had this perception that we were going to visit *poor people.* But I quickly found out that they're just *people.* They were intelligent, capable, and very knowledgeable about the world. The first thing you notice about them is that they are so full of joy. They are very generous. Everywhere we went we were treated like the pope's entourage. They all wanted to share with you, like a farmer offering you a piece of sugar cane.

They put our schedule out on the diocesan radio station and people would walk for hours, sometimes overnight, to meet with us or celebrate Mass with us. It was a very humbling experience. We'd go to a town, and the high school band would be out in the hot sun waiting to play for us. The whole town would be there.

As a cherry farmer, Nita felt a special bond with the coffee producers. Much of their daily life was similar — farmers even called the coffee fruit "cherries"! Although she did not speak Spanish, Nita found that with an interpreter's help she was able to connect deeply with the Nicaraguan farmers. Some conversations felt all-too familiar:

When we were sitting around at dinner, I felt like I was at home talking to an older cherry farmer. He was saying the same things that I hear here. Like, "Oh, this young generation!

They don't know what real work is!" I had asked him what would happen to his ranch when he got older. He said, "Oh, the kids, they won't be able to do it!" I thought, "Okay, you're just like one of these stubborn farmers that I work with."

One of the most moving points of the visit for Nita occurred midway through the trip. Delegates from the Diocese of Gaylord sat in a circle together with CECOSEMAC farmers from a rural area near Matagalpa. The farmers began to tell their stories of Nicaragua's civil war. Equal numbers introduced themselves saying, "I was Contra," or "I was Sandinista." They spoke about their experience of the war and of building peace through farming together in the cooperative.

Nita asked how the farmers could even sit with a group of U.S. citizens, when the United States had supported one side during the war. Without exception, they replied, "That was the U.S. government, not the people." Nita said that the Gaylord delegation was impressed with this reasoned response. "We all said, 'We don't know if we would be that rational about it, if some country had been that involved in something that harmed us so much.'" Their experience of reconciliation is one of the resources the Matagalpans have brought to the partnership.

Such interchanges underscore the reciprocal nature of the CRS-brokered partnership. I asked both Nita and Fr. Walt what they thought Gaylord Catholics had received from the Matagalpans. They cited appreciation for personal qualities like generosity and spirituality, the way that Nicaraguan Catholics express "their dependence on the Lord," and their clear commitment to the common good. Nita was especially taken by the follow-through and accountability within the Nicaraguan church, qualities she does not always find in U.S. churches.

The Nicaraguans serving on the partnership committee in Matagalpa also see the relationship as one that flows both ways. Fr. Ramiro Tijerino, former director of Caritas-Matagalpa, believes:

The partnership is above a material or economic exchange. It's about faith; it's about culture. We have a lot to offer —

our spirituality, the lay participation, our movements, our pilgrimages, our success in promoting vocations. When the delegation from Michigan came down, they were surprised to see all of the young priests here because they don't have any young priests!

As in the Dioceses Without Borders partnership (chapter 1), both sides in this relationship credit the other for shaking up stereotypes. Verónica Alvarez, who chairs the partnership in the Diocese of Matagalpa, had the impression that U.S. citizens were indifferent to the suffering of the poor in other countries, but "they weren't like that," she said. "They asked us, 'How can we help?' We sold out all our coffee!"

Coffee sales are a desired outcome of the partnership, but the time that Matagalpans and Gaylord Catholics spend face-to-face sharing their faith has an even more profound effect. Reflecting on his experience of the early days of the partnership, Archbishop Brenes chuckled, remembering a perception he set out to reverse:

> Some people from Gaylord thought that the Diocese of Mata-galpa wanted to have this relationship in order to request lots of money. The day that we had the first meeting, we didn't present any proposals for money. Rather it was a time to share experiences as church. This went on to the point that they asked us, "What can we help you out with?" But this was not something that we were prepared to do at that point, to ask them for money.

Eyes twinkling, Archbishop Brenes explained that he aimed to teach that solidarity begins with the sharing of faith and culture by delaying any material requests. For Nita and others from the Diocese of Gaylord, this approach has worked. Purchasing coffee in the churches of Gaylord is an act now done with a consciousness of every step of the supply chain, from the "stubborn farmer" picking the cherries to Chris roasting and grinding the beans, to Nita's purchase in the vestibule of St. Michael the Archangel Church.

*Every cup of coffee has a story.* Many Catholics in the Diocese of Gaylord and around the United States now understand the story within their coffee cup because of CRS-Nicaragua's coffee project. It is the life story of Oscar, Dolores, and José, who farm the coffee. It is also an account of Raúl, Sue, and Chris's efforts to perfect the coffee's taste and sell it to U.S. consumers. It is the story of Catholic Relief Services, developing the resources of low-income farmers in a war-weary nation, uniting producers and consumers to concretize the solidarity economy, making visible global supply chains and demonstrating that a decision as simple as what coffee to purchase can be an act of solidarity that transforms the world.

---

### For Reflection

*Every perspective on economic life that is human, moral, and Christian must be shaped by three questions: What does the economy do for people? What does it do to people? And how do people participate in it?* (USCCB, *Economic Justice for All*, no. 1)

+ How can U.S. Catholics use their economic resources to address the three questions posed by the U.S. Catholic bishops?

Please go on-line to *www.storiesofhope.crs.org* for a comprehensive study guide.

# Afterword

As the international humanitarian relief, development, and social justice organization of the U.S. Catholic community, Catholic Relief Services saves lives, relieves suffering, and rebuilds communities in ninety-nine countries around the world. For six decades, we have helped to address the effects of natural disasters, offered treatment and hope in the wake of devastating pandemic diseases such as HIV/AIDS and malaria, and worked to bring peace and reconciliation to communities in conflict.

While most of our work is overseas, our mission also calls us to serve here at home by helping Catholics to live their faith more fully. Following the 2000 World Summit that gathered staff, partners, and supporters to develop a new strategic plan, Catholic Relief Services underwent a profound change. We set out in pursuit of a new and challenging vision for the future — a vision of global solidarity. This vision represents CRS's highest and best dream for a world free from the devastating effects of poverty, conflict, and injustice. It is our vision of a world where everyone, rich and poor alike, lives as brothers and sisters, and the dignity of every person is respected. CRS's U.S. Operations Division was formed in the fall of 2002 to achieve that vision.

The mission of U.S. Operations is to help Catholics respond to the call of the Gospel to live as one human family. Our goal is to help change the hearts, minds, and lives of U.S. Catholics so that, on the basis of faith, Catholics take actions that positively change the lives of people around the world who are afflicted by poverty, disease, conflict, and injustice. We want to create a Catholic movement for global peace and social justice.

Grounded in the principles of Catholic social teaching, CRS accomplishes this mission by building bridges of understanding and partnership, by raising awareness about issues of international peace and social justice, and by advocacy for those whose voices are not heard. We help Catholics in the United States become more informed, energized catalysts, working to eliminate the very systems and structures that keep people in poverty, hamper peaceful societies, and prevent fair and equitable treatment.

Jesus tells us by word and example that true Christian living requires dialogue and engagement with the culture in which we live. Commitment to peace and social justice, exercising a preferential option for the world's poor, respecting the life and dignity of every human person across the full spectrum of life, are the litmus tests of our lives as Jesus' disciples. It is how we will be judged on the last day. Shouldn't we begin now to think, speak, and act differently?

How can we change the way we consume, invest, vote, and give so that the lives of those who are poor and marginalized around the world are improved? What can *we*, the U.S. Catholic community, do to educate others about the global demands of our faith?

Programs like the Catholic Relief Services Africa Campaign, our Fair Trade Coffee, Chocolate, and Handcrafts projects, Operation Rice Bowl, the Legislative Network, and the Volunteer Corps provide concrete opportunities for U.S. Catholics to put our faith into action through these programs which combine catechesis and social analysis and expose participants to the challenges and problems faced by people overseas. In the context of culture, economics, and sociopolitical environments, we help people analyze why problems exist and their impact on all of our lives. Using Scripture and Catholic social teaching, we invite deep reflection on these problems in light of the demands of the Gospel and Jesus' universal call to love of neighbor. Through partnerships with U.S. and overseas dioceses, colleges and universities, seminaries, and other Catholic organizations here and abroad, we put a human face on global issues. Finally, we help people embrace the ministry of peace and justice, which is the responsibility of all who call themselves followers of Christ, and decide what they can do to make a difference.

Catholic Relief Services believes that solidarity will transform not only the lives of poor people overseas, but our own lives as well, we are convinced. A firm commitment to respect the sacredness and dignity of every human being, to share the goods of the earth equitably, to practice peace, justice, and reconciliation, and to cherish and protect the integrity of all creation will fundamentally change the lives of everyone on earth. God has given the human race the ability to achieve such change. Indeed, we are called to be agents of that transformation, to be co-creators of the reign of God on earth. Our duty as Christians is to put our faith into action beyond the limits of our families, neighborhoods, cities, even countries. As members of the universal church, we have the ability to globalize solidarity. With more than 65 million Catholics in the United States, clearly we *can* make a difference for the better. And because we can, we must!

But our collective consciences must be raised. Our awareness of global issues must be increased. We cannot act if we do not know what to do. We must educate ourselves, pass on our knowledge, and get involved.

Over the last sixty-three years, Catholic Relief Services has learned some valuable lessons. One of them is that while relief and development work is essential, it is not enough to permanently change the conditions of poor and suffering people abroad. What the world also needs is a commitment to live as sisters and brothers in the family of God. Because of our work overseas and here at home, Catholic Relief Services, in service to the U.S. Catholic community, is uniquely positioned to help make that commitment a reality.

*Solidarity Will Transform the World: Stories of Hope from Catholic Relief Services* describes some of the many ways to get involved with us in the mission of living in solidarity with our brothers and sisters overseas. It tells the stories of people whose lives have been changed for the better, both here at home and abroad. We hope it will challenge you to respond to Jesus' call to love our neighbors wherever they are by changing the way you live, consume, vote, and give. Finally, we hope it will inspire you to join us as an informed advocate for international peace and social justice and to encourage others to do the same. Together we can make a profound difference in the lives of so many people who are challenged by poverty and injustice beyond our borders. Living as one human family, we can and *will* transform the world!

*Joan Neal*
Executive Vice President,
U.S. Operations, Catholic Relief Services

# Notes

## Introduction

1. This SportAid public service announcement won a Gold Medal at the 1986 International Film and Television Festival of New York. SportAid was a 1986 athletic fundraiser benefiting Ethiopian famine victims organized by musician Bob Geldof, best known for producing the 1985 LiveAid music festival.

2. It would be unfair to suggest that all other relief and development organizations still rely solely on shock-value advertising to generate contributions. Yet some still do, and the U.S. cultural consciousness has been indelibly shaped by such images, even if other relief and development organizations have evolved.

3. John Carr, speech at the U.S. Conference of Catholic Bishops Annual Catholic Social Ministry Gathering, Washington, DC, February 21, 2005.

4. Paul VI, 1967 papal encyclical (a teaching letter) *On the Development of Peoples,* no. 14.

5. Ibid., no. 19.

6. Ibid., no. 21.

7. World Synod of Bishops, *Justice in the World,* no. 71.

8. Ibid.

9. Ibid., no. 59.

10. Ibid., no. 42.

11. For a full introduction to Catholic social teaching and its core themes, see Thomas Massaro, SJ, *Living Justice: Catholic Social Teaching in Action* (Franklin, WI: Sheed & Ward, 2000), and Kenneth R. Himes, OFM, *Responses to 101 Questions on Catholic Social Teaching* (Mahwah, NJ: Paulist Press, 2001). A comprehensive description of CRS's guiding principles and their roots in Catholic social teaching can be found at *www.crs.org/about_us/who_we_are/what_we_believe.cfm.*

12. Massaro, *Living Justice.*

13. *Catechism of the Catholic Church,* no. 1939.

14. Ibid., no. 1941.

15. Ronald Rolheiser, OMI, "Advent Hope," December 3, 2004, accessed on-line on September 9, 2006, at *www.the-tidings.com/2004/1203/ rolheiser.htm.*

16. Archbishop Charles Chaput, "Political Conversation and Witnesses to Belief," *Origins* 35, no. 4 (June 9, 2005): 60–61.

17. Ibid.

### Chapter 1: The Golden Kernel

1. For example, water costs are high ($25 a month or more) because *colonia* residents must purchase potable water in jugs and large containers of water for washing from commercial trucks. Grocery prices at small supermarkets are nearly always higher than at the Wal-Mart in nearby Nogales, Arizona.

2. Reuters, "Bush Blames Democrats for Stalled Immigration Reform," *New York Times,* April 9, 2006.

3. Mark Mather, Kerri L. Rivers, and Linda Jacobsen, "What the American Community Survey Tells Us about U.S. Immigration," *The American Community Survey* (Washington, DC: Population Reference Bureau, 2005).

4. Ginger Thompson, "Migrant Deaths at Record on U.S. Border," *New York Times,* October 5, 2005.

5. The same nickname is also applied to those who smuggle migrants across the Mexican border into the United States for profit.

6. A voucher system ensures that the funds are used for the intended purpose.

7. Oxygen is the primary source of apple decay. If you cut an apple in half, it quickly turns brown. That is oxygen at work. Even with its protective peel, an apple is vulnerable to gradual decay caused by exposure to oxygen. Atmospherically controlled cold storage facilities protect apples by reducing oxygen levels.

8. JustFaith is a thirty-week social justice formation program profiled in Jeffry Odell Korgen, *My Lord and My God: Engaging Catholics in Social Ministry* (Mahwah, NJ: Paulist Press, 2007).

9. Order information is available at *www.crs.org/dramaproject.*

## Chapter 2. The Lazarus Effect

1. While less expensive than the American drugs, generic Indian ARVs have a higher rate of reported side effects, some of which lead patients to discontinue their medication.

2. According to the World Health Organization, 1.1 million Zambians are living with HIV. Ten percent of this group show signs of full-blown AIDS. HIV (Human Immunodeficiency Virus) causes AIDS, a collection of immune system problems known collectively as Acquired Immune Deficiency Syndrome (World Health Organization, "Country Profiles," *2006 Report on the Global AIDS Epidemic*. Accessed on August 28, 2006 at *www.who.int/hiv/mediacentre/2006_GR_ANN1M-Z_en.pdf.*)

3. A "compound" is a group of homes typically surrounded by a protective brick wall. A compound is similar to what we would call a neighborhood or subdivision in the United States, only with brick walls around it.

4. Vulnerable children are those whose parents are living with HIV.

5. All CRS HIV/AIDS prevention and treatment work is guided by Catholic social and moral teachings. A provision in the PEPFAR legislation prohibits discrimination against faith-based organizations on the basis of these teachings.

6. Bills in the House of Representatives and the Senate are numbered when introduced. House bills always begin with H.R., Senate bills with S.

7. To save time when lopsided votes are expected, the leadership of the House and the Senate may call for a voice vote. Members shout "Aye" and "No" just as they might at a local civic meeting.

8. In FY (fiscal year) 2005, Congress funded PEPFAR with $1,273,920,000. In FY 2006, $1,975,050,000. In FY 2007, the funding increased to $3.25 billion. President Bush has requested $4.15 billion for FY 2008.

## Chapter 3: A New Awakening

1. While their numbers are small nationwide, Santals are the largest indigenous tribal group in India and quite numerous in the state of West Bengal, where many of these interviews took place.

2. In *Modern Catholic Social Teaching: The Popes Confront the Industrial Age 1740–1958* (New York: Paulist Press, 2003), Joseph Holland

reveals that over a century before Pope Leo XIII's "first" Catholic social teaching encyclical, usury was the church's highest priority in terms of economic justice.

3. Single women typically leave their village after marriage, so they are encouraged to wait until they are fully settled before joining a group.

4. Jack Weatherford, *The History of Money* (New York: Three Rivers Press, 1997), describes the use of "commodity money" prior to the development of metal and paper currency. Aztecs used cacao beans, Guatemalans used corn, Mongolians bricks of tea, Norwegians butter. In Japan, "standardized measures of rice traditionally served as commodity money." In twenty-first-century India, villagers have reintroduced commodity money as a steppingstone toward developing cash assets (20).

5. CRS works with global economic experts to determine microenterprise projects with the greatest likelihood of success. For example, it makes no sense to encourage villagers to make soap if large manufacturers can do it more cheaply and undercut them in price.

6. CRS is one of many organizations developing self-help groups in India. In total, over 1 million self-help groups exist on the subcontinent, composed of over 17 million members. For a technical comparison of how these groups operate, with particular reference to the work of Catholic Relief Services, see Kim Wilson, "The New Microfinance: An Essay on the Self-Help Group Movement in India," *Journal of Microfinance* 4, no. 2 (Fall 2002): 217–45.

7. Participation of women in local governance is guided by the Seventy-Third Amendment to the PRI Act, which now reserves one-third of all local governance seats for women. Self-help groups provide an entry-level platform for women to enter public life. I observed the effects of other amendments to PRI legislation while traveling in these villages. For example, members of one group explained that they had not elected anyone to the PRI because all of the seats had been reserved for another caste (a racial/ethnic/class grouping) for the next five years.

8. Paul VI, *On the Development of Peoples,* no. 87.

9. See Ashutosh Varshney, *Ethnic Conflict and Civic Life: Hindus and Muslims in India* (New Haven, CT: Yale University Press, 2002), for more on Hindu/Muslim conflict in India.

## Chapter 4: Forgiving the Unforgivable

1. From 1916 to 1959, following the teachings of European anthropologists, the Belgians favored the taller, thinner, and lighter-skinned Tutsis (14 percent of the population) over the shorter, darker Hutus (85 percent of the population). The Belgians set up a Tutsi monarch to rule the country for them with a Tutsi court and bureaucracy. In the 1930s, the Belgians introduced ethnic identity cards to enforce the physical distinctions. Fueled by United Nations pressure on Belgium to institute democracy, a Hutu rebellion broke out in 1959, leading 150,000 Tutsis to flee to neighboring countries. Independence from Belgium and revolution brought Hutus to power in Rwanda in 1962. Over the next three decades, Rwandan life was characterized by sporadic massacres of Tutsis and the exclusion of Tutsis from government jobs. For further reading on the Rwandan genocide and its roots in the colonial experience, see General Romeo Dallaire, *Shake Hands with the Devil: The Failure of Humanity in Rwanda* (New York: Carroll and Graf, 2003), and Philip Gourevitch, *We Wish to Inform You That Tomorrow We Will Be Killed with Our Families* (New York: Farrar, Straus and Giroux, 1998).

2. Animators of base communities are lay people of exceptional faith who receive special training as catechists. They organize weekly meetings of their base community and lead discussions connecting faith and life experience.

3. The idea of truth-telling as a first step to peace was pioneered by the post-apartheid Truth and Reconciliation Commission of South Africa, led by Anglican Archbishop Desmond Tutu and utilized by other nations after civil wars. For further reading, see Russell Daye, *Political Forgiveness: Lessons from South Africa* (Maryknoll, NY: Orbis Books, 2004).

4. Rwanda has released confessing prisoners due to illness, age, or half of sentence served in groups of forty thousand at a time.

5. Clergy shortages in Rwanda led to the development of subparishes, typically led by lay catechists. Subparishes gather for prayer without Eucharist three out of four Sundays. Lay "animators" like Modeste lead base communities, an even smaller unit of parish life composed of twenty-five families.

6. RPF leader Paul Kagame, now president of Rwanda, believed that the first step toward rebuilding the country was encouraging ordinary people to resume their lives at home as quickly as possible.

7. Modeste is also a singer-songwriter who has written songs about the genocide and reconciliation. Two of his songs can be heard at *www.storiesofhope.crs.org.*

8. Ntarama Church is now a major genocide memorial. Most of the bodies have been buried on the church grounds. Inside the sanctuary, fifty skulls are neatly arranged on shelves, indicating the various ways victims were killed, and bags of bones mark every corner of the church. Holes in the brick mark where soldiers threw grenades into the church, before finishing their work with machetes. The tin roof is pocked with shrapnel holes. The holes are so numerous that a new exterior roof has been built three feet above the old one to prevent rainwater from dripping inside. A large banner outside proclaims, in Kinyarwanda, "If you knew yourself, and if you knew who I was, you would not have killed me."

9. Murder Victims' Families for Human Rights is an international, non-governmental organization of family members of victims of criminal murder, terrorist killings, state executions, extrajudicial assassinations, and "disappearances" working to oppose the death penalty from a human rights perspective. Membership is open to all victims' family members who oppose the death penalty in all cases. *www.willsworld.com/~mvfhr/.*

10. Pseudonym.

11. "Respect for and development of human life require peace. Peace is not merely the absence of war, and it is not limited to maintaining a balance of powers between adversaries. Peace cannot be attained on earth without safeguarding the goods of persons, free communication among men, respect for the dignity of persons and peoples, and the assiduous practice of fraternity. Peace is 'the tranquility of order.' Peace is the work of justice and the effect of charity" (*Catechism of the Catholic Church,* no. 2304).

## Chapter 5: The Solidarity Economy

1. From the moment that former dictator Anastasio Somoza was deposed in 1979 until a cease fire was signed in 1988, Nicaraguans lived in a state of civil war between the Marxist Sandinista government and

resistance fighters known as Contras, who originally represented those who benefited from the dictatorship but enlarged in the late 1980s to include others disaffected with the Sandinista revolution. The Reagan administration supported the Contras during the war, often covertly and sometimes infamously (the "Iran-Contra Affair" of the late 1980s was a major government scandal).

2. Alfonso Cotera Fretal, *Local Solidarity in Microfinance: Study of Experiences in Peru, Ecuador, Brazil, and Haiti*, Latin American and Caribbean Network of Catholic Institutions with Programs in Microfinance, 2003.

3. For more information about the Fair Trade Labeling Organization, see *www.fairtrade.net*.

4. A film describing the coffee production process is available on-line at *www.storiesofhope.crs.org*.

5. For further information about ecotourism opportunities in Nicaragua, go to *www.storiesofhope.crs.org*.

6. The *Journal of Food Science* has published a peer-reviewed paper on this experiment: Susan C. Jackels and Charles F. Jackels, "Characterization of the Coffee Mucilage Fermentation Process Using Chemical Indicators: A Field Study in Nicaragua," *Journal of Food Science* 70 (2005): C321–C325.

7. On the other hand, CRS and many other organizations involved with Fair Trade coffee applaud Wal-Mart's entry into Fair Trade coffee sales. If the demand for fairly traded coffee is to be substantially enlarged, the participation of major retailers like Wal-Mart is essential.